COMPOSE YOURSELF!

A GUIDE TO CRITICAL THINKING AND

ANALYTICAL WRITING IN SECONDARY SCHOOL

Amy Rukea Stempel

This edition published by
Dog Ear Publishing
4010 W. 86th Street, Ste H
Indianapolis, IN 46268

www.dogearpublishing.net

ISBN: 978-160844-645-2
This book is printed on acid-free paper.

Printed in the United States of America

WITH GRATITUDE

This book would not have been possible without the frustrations, hard questions, and ultimate successes of my students. Many thanks for letting me work with you over the years.

Profound thanks also go to my editors, Stephanie Soper and Nancy Dean, and writing mentors, Dr. Ruth Mitchell and Patte Barth. A writer is only as good as her teachers.

And finally, a shout out to my family, husband and daughter, who have endured many, many hours, days, years of my somewhat obsessive interests. You both keep me sane.

TABLE OF CONTENTS

It goes against the grain of modern education to teach students to program [computers]. What fun is there to making plans, acquiring discipline, organizing thoughts, devoting attention to detail, and learning to be self critical?

—Alan Perlis, computer scientist

INTRODUCTION

BEFORE WRITING BEGINS

GETTING STARTED: THE PIECES OF AN ANALYTICAL ESSAY

THE MANY PIECES BECOME A WHOLE

THINKING & ORGANIZATION TOOLBOX

RUBRICS FOR ASSESSMENT

WRITING IN ALL SUBJECTS

GO FORTH AND PROSPER

BLACK-LINE MASTERS   AVAILABLE ONLINE @ WWW.LIGHTBULBLEARNING.NET
CLICK "PUBLICATIONS"

- ❖ Organization Template
- ❖ Editing Checklist
- ❖ Compare-Contrast Analysis Organizer
- ❖ Cause-Effect Analysis Organizer
- ❖ Problem-Solution Analysis Organizer
- ❖ Concept-Definition Analysis Organizer
- ❖ Goal-Action-Outcome Analysis Organizer
- ❖ Proposition-Support Analysis Organizer
- ❖ Lab Report Template
- ❖ Rubric

WRITING SAMPLES   AVAILABLE ONLINE @ WWW.LIGHTBULBLEARNING.NET
CLICK "PUBLICATIONS"

INTRODUCTION

Why Require Analytical Writing in All Subjects?

Organizing is what you do before you do something, so that when you do it, it is not all mixed up.

—A.A. Milne

Writing is thinking made visible. Unclear writing reflects unclear thinking. Students tell their teachers and parents, "I know the answer, I just can't explain it!" or "I don't care if you don't understand what I've written, I know what I mean!" While these responses can be exasperating, they also bode ill for students' future success. School is where students need to learn how to structure and communicate their analytical thinking. And analytical writing is the most effective means for schools to teach students how to do that. This resource guide can be the first step on that path.

Much has been written about the creative aspect of writing narratives; however, there has been relatively little focus on the types of expository academic writing students need in order to succeed both in school and later in life. Schools explicitly teach narrative, descriptive writing beginning in elementary school. Unfortunately, too often educators then expect secondary students will intuit how to transfer those skills to write clear, concise, organized responses to difficult, real-world questions in secondary school. When this does not happen, parents and teachers wonder why students are not able to analyze and synthesize information effectively.

Generally, our society thinks of writing as a creative art, not a learned, structured skill. However, in order for others to follow one's thinking in all disciplines, ideas need to be logically organized and effectively communicated. Individuals cannot think clearly without using well-ordered language, let alone communicate with others.

While there are detailed books teaching analytical thinking and writing, such as *St. Martin's Guide to Writing (9th Edition)* by Rise B. Axelrod and *Critical Strategies for Academic Thinking & Writing* by Mike Ross & Malcolm Kiniry, **Compose Yourself!** is designed to be a quick and easy guide to teaching and learning critical thinking and analytical writing at the secondary level. I recommend that all secondary teachers use this resource as the basic framework when analytical writing is called for in each subject area. Ideally, all teachers at a school will work from this framework so that the faculty can develop a common language and expectation for writing and thinking instruction. However, even if schools choose not to use this guide, parents and students can do so independently to help strengthen thinking and writing skills. In the process, students will learn how to better retain information, leading to improved overall academic performance.

Encouraging <u>Intellectual</u> Creativity

Intellectual creativity is not "anything goes." Albert Einstein had to work within, and explain, the known rules of the universe before he could convince other scientists of the validity of the Theory of Relativity. Truly creative people do not—in fact they cannot—ignore the realities in which they find themselves. What they do is interpret and make connections between and among facts and disciplines in ways that no one else has done before.

Most critically, those who are intellectually creative—or at least those who make their mark on the world—are able to effectively communicate that interpretation to others. No matter how brilliant the person, if she cannot communicate her thinking to the wider world, nothing will come of it.

Unfortunately, research shows that students in the United States are weak when it comes to reading and writing non-fiction, as is apparent in the results of the National Assessment of Educational Progress (NAEP). This is <u>not</u> because students cannot learn these skills, but because we so often do not teach it well, or at all. (For more information on NAEP go to: http://nces.ed.gov/nationsreportcard/)

Narrative vs. Analytical (Expository) Writing

Students begin learning to write in elementary school by composing personal narratives. It is the way the human brain is naturally wired to work—to tell a story. However, academic writing that explains the relationships and patterns between and among ideas is analytical and expository. Analytical writing and thinking is the currency of the academic world. It is also the currency of the real world. Colleagues do not want a story (i.e., a narrative) about the workshop. They want an analysis of what worked, what didn't work, and what changes need to be made to make it better.

Thinking Made Visible

Narrative	Expository
❖ Can be fiction or non-fiction	❖ Provides information and analysis; is non-fiction
❖ Follows a "story" structure (beginning-middle-end)	❖ Analyzes existing facts and ideas for relationships and patterns
❖ Uses sensory descriptions and images to engage all the senses	❖ Employs one of the six analytical text structures
❖ Is taught first because the human brain is naturally wired to tell stories	❖ Is organized logically with clear thesis, supporting ideas, and supporting evidence
❖ Is used often in the early grades to learn about the craft of literary, descriptive writing	❖ Forces writer to think about thinking (metacognition)
❖ Can be fictitious; no command of the facts necessary	❖ Must have supporting ideas and evidence that demonstrate a command of the facts
	❖ Represents abstract thinking rather than sensory understanding

 The purposes and methods of organization in narrative and analytical writing are very different. There can be a transfer in style and descriptive detail between these two types of writing, but it must not interfere with the text's organization.

Teaching & Measuring Student Thinking

The *only* way to adequately teach "higher-order thinking" or "critical thinking" and ensure students' enduring capacity for it is through the written analysis of facts and data. We know it works; so why do we avoid it? It takes discipline, deep knowledge, and constant reflection on the part of *both* teachers and students. Easily said, less easily done. This book will help teachers teach and students learn how to think critically and write analytically in all subject areas, as well as help students develop the deep knowledge and skills required to succeed. By using a framework, it is possible to begin to develop the discipline required to be critical thinkers.

Formulaic vs. Structured Writing

In architecture, laws of gravity, force, and stress, as well as the functions the building will fulfill, must be the primary basis for its design. If these laws and needs are not followed, the building runs the risk of falling apart and failing in its mission. Still, there is room for a great deal of creativity and original expression within the limits set by these laws and needs. Heeding the laws that provide for a solid, functional structure need not mean following a "formula."

It is the same with critical thinking and analytical writing. Following rules for good structure helps to lead an audience through the thinking within a text so that it can follow its logic and understand how its ideas relate to one another. With sophisticated, complex, and transparent transitional language—that is the language that represents the writer's logic and analysis—there is no need for formulaic writing. An analytical text can adhere to good structure *and* be creative.

There is no need, then, to avoid teaching structure out of concern for squelching students' creativity. In fact, as in architecture, a developing writer must *first* learn the rules of structure. This book is designed to guide teachers as they develop in their students the structured skills of thinking and writing. Upcoming supplements will help teachers deepen this instruction.

Formal vs. Informal Writing

Academic writing is formal writing. That does not mean it has to be boring or in-comprehensible; however, secondary students should *not* write like they speak. There are a few basic, common sense guidelines for formal, analytical, academic writing that all students should follow:

- ❖ Remove first and second person references (no "*I*" or "*you*");

- ❖ Remove slang, "text," or internet spelling or vocabulary;

- ❖ Remove contractions;

- ❖ Remove "chatty" or familiar tone. Rather than, ~~Let me tell you about photosynthesis~~, write, "Photosynthesis is the process by which plants convert sunlight into food";

- ❖ Remove imprecise or over-generalized vocabulary, such as *like, stuff, a lot, thing, very, something, everything, always, never, you know, whatever, it* (with no clear antecedent);

- ❖ Remove unnecessary repetition; and

- ❖ Remove emotional responses to content. Rather than, ~~I liked this book~~, determine what you liked about it. What were the specific criteria that determined whether or not you liked it? Did it have a fast-paced plot, well-developed characters, or an unusual theme? If so, write, This book is one of the best releases this spring because it has a fast-paced plot, well-developed characters, and an unusual theme. Continue by explaining and illustrating this thesis in the body of the essay with examples from the book.

There are very few exceptions to these guidelines, and it is important for students to learn them early and follow them consistently.

What Not to Worry About

Non-language arts teachers often become nervous when they learn they are supposed to teach writing. This attitude is based on a misunderstanding of what "writing" is. Since writing is thinking made visible, educators in all subject areas teach thinking and all should also use and teach analytical writing. This is critically different than narrative, creative, or literary writing. It is not a science teacher's job to nurture the next James Joyce, but to develop students who can clearly read, think, and write "science."

What does this mean? Non-language arts teachers are *not* responsible for teaching the following:

❖ **Grammar, usage, mechanics, and spelling (except for subject-specific vocabulary):** It is only fair to students to circle any mistakes a teacher sees in their grammar, usage, mechanics, and spelling so they have some sense of how much work they have to do. However, non-language arts teachers do not have to read closely for it (if a few mistakes are missed, so be it), do not have to factor it into the grade, and do not have to teach it in their classroom.

❖ **Style and voice:** Good expository writing exudes style and voice; however, subject-area teachers are not responsible for teaching these skills. The ability to write clearly with style across the curriculum comes with practice, combined with spiraled instruction in the language arts classroom.

❖ **"Literary" narrative writing:** Artistic, creative writing has no place in the other subject areas. See the discussion of intellectual creativity versus artistic creativity earlier in this section.

That said, what are non-language teachers responsible for when teaching thinking and writing? They are responsible for those elements of writing that reflect thinking in their subject areas:

- ❖ **Thesis statements:** Students need modeling and direct instruction in the kinds of thesis statements that are appropriate in each subject area. This is how students learn the "higher-order" thinking they will need to succeed in that subject area.

- ❖ **Structure and organization:** What supporting evidence is relevant to the thesis? How is it communicated in that subject area? How does one judge the appropriateness and relevance of supporting ideas and evidence in a particular subject area?

- ❖ **Transition words and phrases:** Transition language communicates to the reader how the ideas are related and how they connect to other knowledge and disciplines. Therefore, transitions need to be explicitly taught and then required in student writing throughout the disciplines.

- ❖ **Content and content area vocabulary:** What are the knowledge and facts upon which students will base their thinking and writing? Of course, subject-area teachers are responsible for determining how best to teach this to students.

Please remember, when educators are learning to teach something new and when students are learning a new skill, it takes much longer than everyone would like to become fluent in the process, and the quality of the initial products may leave something to be desired.

Perhaps an analogy will help. Think about anything new you recently learned to do. For me, it was learning how to knit. At first, each step—casting on, knitting each row, etc.—took forever, the product looked a bit forlorn, and I despaired as to whether or not I would ever be able to knit without consulting the directions and concentrating intensely. It will be some time before I can knit while chatting with friends or watching T.V. Similarly, learning to teach writing and thinking will take time. The good news is that as teachers and students become more proficient, less instructional time will be required, and student products will improve significantly—especially if all teachers in the school require their students to write. And the truth is that actively requiring and teaching analytical writing within the subject areas is the only way to both teach and measure the quality of students' critical, high-order thinking.

However, to improve knowledge of general grammar and usage rules, the following resources are helpful:

- ❖ *English Grammar For Dummies* by Geraldine Woods (also available: *English Grammar Workbook For Dummies,* a companion book with quizzes and worksheets)

- ❖ *Elements of Style* by Strunk & White

- ❖ *Grammar Girl's Quick and Dirty Tips for Better Writing* by Mignon Fogarty

- ❖ *The Grammar Devotional: Daily Tips for Successful Writing from Grammar Girl* by Mignon Fogarty

- ❖ *The Blue Book of Grammar and Punctuation: An Easy-to-Use Guide with Clear Rules, Real-World Examples, and Reproducible Quizzes* by Jane Straus

- ❖ *Mechanically Inclined: Building Grammar, Usage, and Style into Writer's Workshop* by Jeff Anderson

The *Compose Yourself!* Mantra

Writing is thinking made visible. Not writing clearly means one is not thinking clearly. Analysis is a learned skill. Everyone can learn how to do it with the right instruction. Following the steps in this guide will lead to disciplined thinking and writing.

That which we persist in doing becomes easier for us to do; not that the nature of the thing itself is changed, but that our power to do so is increased.

—Heber J. Grant

We are what we repeatedly do. Excellence, therefore, is not an act but a habit.

– Aristotle

This resource is best used by a teacher (or parent) to guide students as they learn how to think and write analytically. It is meant to inform the academic writing students are assigned in school, not to require additional work. The goal is to help students improve their analytical, academic writing (that is, expository writing) and to bolster subject-area instruction. **Compose Yourself!** will benefit all sixth, seventh, eighth, and ninth grade teachers, parents, and students. In addition, it will improve the skills of those tenth, eleventh, and twelfth grade students who are struggling writers as well as those who persistently underachieve.

Each adult/student pair or class can begin by reading each section together and spending a day or two looking for examples in their own reading and previous writing. Don't rush it.

For example, read the section on *Text Structures* and then examine any analytical, expository writing at home or school to determine its text structure (e.g., textbooks, newspapers, magazines, non-fiction books, and/or prior analytical essays). If the student has an analytical writing assignment pending, ask which text structure would be the most logical way to organize the written response.

Go through each section this way. Again, after reading the section on *Thesis Statements*, check any expository texts in the classroom or home to determine if they include a strong thesis statement and what it is.

Each section is purposely short so that the teacher and student can concentrate on learning one concept at a time. It will take a while for students to learn to integrate them seamlessly. In fact, the only way it will happen is to engage in the cycle of practice, feedback (grades, comments, peer editing, etc.), practice, and more feedback. There is no way to learn to do it well immediately. However, following the steps outlined in this guide will certainly speed up the process significantly.

Finally, focus on an actual class assignment. The content of the assigned writing/thinking could be anything—history, literature, science, math, art, health—but the organization will, for the time being, look like what is outlined here. Students should use the *Toolbox* section beginning on page 85 of this guide. They can follow the *Order of Operations* (on page 85) and transfer information from the appropriate *Analysis Organizer* to the writing template provided (on page 86).

Of course, structure and organization are not everything. It is critical that as students put their response together, they focus on transitional words and phrases that best show the relationships between and among their ideas. Unusual connections or a nuanced understanding of the topic always makes for a stronger text. However, without a coherent structure, even the most original thinker will have a hard time communicating with others. Best of all, often the act of organizing the information actually helps the writer to see connections and develop a nuanced understanding of the topic.

So practice away!

Periodic Supplements

In order to help students deepen their understanding of the connection between text structures, writing, and thinking, supplements to this basic guide will be published periodically. This will keep the doses of instruction practical and digestible. Take it one step at a time, access the supplements as needed, and strong thinkers and writers will develop.

Future supplements:

- ❖ Idea combining (often referred to as sentence combining)
- ❖ Integrating quotations into an essay
- ❖ Summarizing expository writing
- ❖ Summarizing narrative writing
- ❖ Writing the perfect college admissions essay

Check **www.lightbulblearning.net** periodically for more news on release dates and additional titles.

Notes

BEFORE WRITING BEGINS

Analysis is about breaking things into their component parts—to their "puzzle pieces"—in order to better understand how to put them back together more effectively. It is possible to analyze ideas ("democracy") or skills ("how to throw a ball"). This guide provides easy steps to improve academic, analytical writing in order to make it better.

Secondary teachers often work with students who are used to writing narratives. Stories, made-up or real; descriptions; even poetry can be narrative. The personal narratives composed in elementary school, although not necessarily fiction, are written in the narrative form, just like fiction. However, very little academic writing is narrative and the academic writing that is narrative, such as case studies, is designed to support an analytical argument.

Students in middle and high school need help structuring their analytical thinking and writing as they are often expected to write about, explain, and analyze fact-based concepts—concepts they can't make up. The reason they are asked to do this is so they can learn and then apply these concepts to future learning. These are the nuggets of knowledge they will use to build their future!

Analytical non-fiction pieces can be divided into six different text structures:

- ❖ **Compare-Contrast:** A compare-contrast essay focuses on the similarities and differences between at least two objects or ideas. The purpose is to develop the relationship between them and, in the process, explain both in detail.

- ❖ **Cause-Effect:** A cause-effect essay first presents a reason or motive for an event, situation, or trend and then explains its result or consequence.

- ❖ **Problem-Solution:** A problem-solution essay informs readers about a complex, real-world, philosophical problem (or related problems), followed by actions that could be taken to remedy the problem.

- ❖ **Concept-Definition (descriptive writing):** A concept-definition essay provides a personal, but still factually complete and correct, understanding of a particular concept or term. The essay conveys what research and experience have taught the writer (what the concept "is not" is often also part of the definition).

- ❖ **Goal-Action-Outcome (process or procedural writing):** A goal-action-outcome essay either tells the reader how to do something or describes how something is done. Math explanations and science lab reports are good examples of goal-action-outcome writing.

- ❖ **Proposition-Support (persuasive writing):** A proposition-support essay uses logic, reason, and supporting data to argue that one idea is more legitimate than another. The argument must include sound reasoning and reliable external evidence, stating facts, giving logical reasons, using examples, and quoting reliable experts and original sources.

All analytical non-fiction, in all subject areas, falls into these six categories. In a longer non-fiction work, such as a book, the author will mix things up, using text structures within text structures. Only when analytical writing includes case studies to illustrate analytical conclusions does it use the narrative structure.

BUT FIRST: Learn how to use each text structure by itself.

All writing begins with a topic—the broad idea the author will address. In order to practice thinking and writing, we need a BIG question, or topic—subject matter that is especially interesting to the writer. That's the first puzzle piece. How about this:

What really caused the loss of life on the Titanic and how have such catastrophes been avoided since?

With all the interest generated by the movie *Titanic*, the story of the luxury liner has been reborn. But did the disaster really unfold the way it is portrayed in the movie? We will thoroughly research this topic while applying critical thinking and, in the process, develop exemplary analytical writing skills.

Similarly, there are myriad BIG questions related to learning in every subject:

- ❖ A science teacher might ask: *How can the school reduce its carbon foot-print?*

- ❖ An English teacher might ask: *Does Odysseus fulfill the role of an ancient Greek hero?*

- ❖ An art teacher might ask: *How do your color choices affect the tone and mood of a piece?*

- ❖ A history/social studies teacher might ask: *What were the major causes of the fall of the Roman Empire?*

The good news is that no matter what the subject matter, the rules governing good analytical writing never change!

Caution: Most of the time topics are phrased as questions, but not always. Sometimes teachers use words like "explain," "analyze," "describe," etc. For example: *"Explain how an author communicates ideas using symbolism."* It is not a question exactly, but it is a vast topic that the writer will need to narrow down in a thesis statement in order to address it effectively.

There is not enough information yet to make a decision about which text structure to use for the *Titanic* topic. However, we can take a minute to think about which text structure would be most helpful for that case as well as each of the additional topics suggested. No final decision is necessary until after the brainstorming and research steps are completed.

POSSIBLE TEXT STRUCTURES

TOPIC	POSSIBLE TEXT STRUCTURE
What really caused the loss of life on the Titanic and how have such catastrophes been avoided since?	Either a proposition-support (provide an opinion, based on research and experience, and support it with evidence and examples) OR straight cause-effect
How can the school reduce its carbon footprint?	Problem-solution OR proposition-support (depending on how much the focus is on explaining the problem of global warming)
How do color choices affect the tone and mood of a piece?	Proposition-support OR concept-definition (depending on whether the focus is on the concept of color [concept-definition] or the development of mood [proposition-support])
Does Odysseus fulfill the role of an ancient Greek hero?	Concept-definition (define concept of an ancient Greek hero using Odysseus as an example or non-example)
What were the major causes of the fall of the Roman Empire?	This one is easy—cause-effect!

EXAMPLES OF TOPICS FOR EACH TEXT STRUCTURE

TEXT STRUCTURE	DEFINITION	EXAMPLES OF TOPICS
Compare-Contrast	A compare-contrast essay focuses on the similarities and differences between at least two objects or ideas. The purpose is to develop the relationship between them and, in the process, explain both in detail.	Compare-contrast how plants and animals respirate. Compare-contrast Oedipus and Creon as leaders. Compare-contrast the major elements in Christianity and Buddhism.
Cause-Effect	A cause-effect essay first presents a reason or motive for an event, situation, or trend and then explains its result or consequence.	How and why do plants grow? How and why do totalitarian governments form?
Problem-Solution	A problem-solution essay informs readers about a complex, real-world, philosophical problem (or related problems), followed by actions that could be taken to remedy the problem.	What should be done about global warming? How can the Federal Reserve help keep economic crises from spinning out of control?

EXAMPLES OF TOPICS FOR EACH TEXT STRUCTURE (CONT.)

TEXT STRUCTURE	DEFINITION	EXAMPLES OF TOPICS
Concept-Definition (descriptive writing)	In a concept-definition essay, the writer provides a personal, but still factually complete and correct, understanding of a particular concept or term. The essay conveys what research and experience have taught the writer (what the concept "is not" is often also part of the definition).	Provide a detailed definition of "democracy". What is figurative language? What is the Greek heroic ideal?
Goal-Action-Outcome (process or procedural writing)	A goal-action-outcome essay either tells the reader how to do something or describes how something is done. Math explanations and science lab reports are good examples of goal-action-outcome writing.	A science lab report An explanation of how to solve a complex, multi-step math problem(s) A business proposal A fitness plan
Proposition-Support (persuasive writing)	A proposition-support essay uses logic, reason, and supporting data to argue that one idea is more legitimate than another. The argument must include sound reasoning and reliable external evidence, stating facts, giving logical reasons, using examples, and quoting reliable experts and original sources.	Are modern values and morals more conservative than those exhibited in the life and times of Henry VIII? Is racism still a problem in this country?

Finding more pieces to the puzzle requires **brainstorming**; that is, thinking about it. When brainstorming, ask questions that can be answered with research. Try to break apart and define the terms in the big question. Think about what questions both you and other interested people might have. In the *Titanic* example, here are some questions we might ask and answer:

What really caused the loss of life on the Titanic and how have such catastrophes been avoided since?	Questions like....

- ❖ Why did the other ships in the area not hit the icebergs?
- ❖ Why did the *Titanic* get so close that it hit the iceberg?
- ❖ What was the exact sequence of events?
- ❖ Is 2.5 hours a long or short time for such a large ship to sink?
- ❖ Could the iceberg have been avoided?
- ❖ Did Captain Smith take *any* precautions?
- ❖ Is there any evidence from the bottom of the sea to help explain what happened?
- ❖ Could the loss of life have been avoided?
- ❖ Was the sinking just bad luck?
- ❖ Why did it take so long to rescue the survivors?
- ❖ Could any ship in the area have reached them sooner?
- ❖ Why were there not enough lifeboats for everyone on board?
- ❖ Based on how it sank, did ship builders and engineers learn anything new?
- ❖ Was the *Titanic* really as strong as the owner said it was?
- ❖ Were any changes made in maritime law and procedure after the accident?

Not all research takes months or weeks to compile. Sometimes research is simply looking up unfamiliar terms and finding evidence from books or articles read in class to support an opinion. Other times, research takes much longer. However, all analytical writing includes at least a little bit of research. There is no way to sit down and write a decent essay from beginning to end without having to find and check facts and quotes—that's research. While a writer's opinions or observations may be part of the answer, they cannot stand alone.

Now, we need to find the answers to our questions by doing the following:

❖ defining any unfamiliar terms;

❖ jotting down any already known answers to questions plus any information that that requires the writer's own specific point of view; and/or

❖ going to the library, web, books, magazines to find reliable expert opinions and research on the topic.

The writer must support his opinions with evidence from others (authors, scientists, other reliable experts, eye-witnesses, etc.)—his opinion alone is not sufficient.

| What really caused the loss of life on the Titanic and how have such catastrophes been avoided since? | Resources found (reported in MLA format):
• Ballard, Robert. <u>Dr. Robert Ballard's Titanic</u>. New York: Barnes & Noble, 2007.
• Matsen, Brad. <u>Titanic's Last Secrets.</u> New York: Twelve, 2008.
• Brown, David. <u>The Last Log of the Titanic</u>. Crawfordsville IN: International Marine, a Division of McGraw-Hill, 2001.
• Lord, Walter. <u>A Night to Remember</u>. New York: Holt, 2005.
• ed. Winocour, Jack. <u>The Story of the Titanic as Told by its Survi-</u> |

vors. Mineola, NY: Dover, 1960.
- Multiple Authors. "Encyclopedia Titanica". 5-April-2010 <http://www.encyclopedia-titanica.org/>.
- Behe, George. "Titanic Inquiry Project". Titanic Inquiry Project. 5-April-2010 <http://www.titanicinquiry.org/>.
- Multiple Authors. "Titanic". Wikipedia. 5-April-2010 <http://en.wikipedia.org/wiki/RMS_Titanic > http://www.uscg-iip.org/
- Multiple Authors. "International Ice Patrol". United States Coast Guard. 5-April-2010 <http://www.uscg-iip.org/cms/ >.

❖ Why did other ships in the area not hit the iceberg?

General maritime custom at that time was to steam full speed until ice was actually sighted. There is always ice in the North Atlantic during April, so the condition was not unusual. At that time, ships communicated informally about ice and danger via telegraph, so all ships, including *Titanic*, knew there was ice. Some ships (the *Californian*) actually stopped dead in the water for the night because the captain thought it was too dangerous to continue. Other ships slowed down. And some ships, including the *Titanic*, did nothing.

❖ Why did the *Titanic* get so close that it hit the iceberg?

No one saw it in time. It was a very clear, calm night with no moon, which actually makes it harder to see icebergs (no chop at the base). Once seen, the officer at the wheel did try to turn the ship, but the ship was so big and moved so slowly that it didn't clear the iceberg in time.

❖ What was the exact sequence of events?

The ship sank in 2 hours and 23 minutes. Immediately after hitting the iceberg, most crew and passengers thought that there was minimal damage. About 20 minutes later, Captain Smith, the ship's designer (Thomas Andrews), and ship's owner (J. Bruce Ismay) knew the ship would sink within an hour-and-a-half. They knew there were not enough lifeboats, so to avoid a panic they never actually told the passengers what was occurring.

❖ Is 2.5 hours a long or short time for such a large ship to sink?

It is extremely fast. No one thought the entire ship could sink so quickly. Prior to the *Titanic* sinking, most large ships that foundered had stayed afloat for a day or two before sinking, allowing passengers to be rescued. Most people thought that large ships effectively acted as their own lifeboats until help could arrive.

❖ Could the iceberg have been avoided?

In hindsight, yes. The binoculars used by the lookouts had been left behind in Southampton, so only human observation was possible. Also, since Captain Smith knew there was ice, he could have reduced speed, which would have given the ship more time to turn once the iceberg was sighted.

❖ Did Captain Smith take *any* precautions?

Yes, Captain Smith adjusted the *Titanic's* course ten miles to the south to avoid the ice he knew about. He ordered the lookouts to watch closely for ice and he closed the forward engine room windows to prevent the glare from interfering with the lookouts' line of sight. The entire crew was alerted to the possibility of ice. But the order to reduce the ship's speed was never given.

❖ Is there any evidence from the bottom of the sea to help explain what happened?

Since the wreck of the *Titanic* was located in 1985, there has been a great deal of on-going research. The most interesting piece of new data has been the idea that the expansion joints on the *Titanic* (two flexible joints that allow the huge steel ship to "flex" in high seas) were a point of weakness and contributed to the breakup of the ship. Since the *Titanic* was the largest ship ever built, even the engineers were not entirely certain their strength calculations were correct. In addition, virtually the entire bottom of the ship was found in August 2005 quite a distance from the main wreck, indicating that it had peeled off on the surface and caused the *Titanic* to quickly sink.

❖ Could the loss of life have been avoided?

Once it hit the iceberg, *Titanic* was doomed. If another ship had been close enough to come to its rescue, then maybe the passengers and crew could have been saved. But this was not to be. When the *Titanic* struck the iceberg and no external rescue was forthcoming, it was inevitable that at least 1,000 people would die, because there were not enough lifeboats. As it turned out, 1,500 people perished because what lifeboats there were did not leave the ship completely full. Had the *Californian* been able to get there in time, some of those 1,500 might have been saved, but the sinking happened so fast, many still would have died. The water was below freezing (salt water has a lower freezing point than regular water). Even with life jackets, no one could survive more than 15 minutes in water that frigid.

❖ Was the sinking just bad luck?

Partly. Many, many things had to go wrong for such a large ship to sink so quickly. The lookouts had no binoculars; the angle of impact was the worst possible; the telegraph operator on the closest ship, the *Californian*, went to bed a few minutes before the *Titanic*'s distress call; the Captain of the *Californian* saw the flares from the *Titanic* but thought they were signal flares because they were white, not red.

❖ Why did it take so long to rescue the survivors?

The telegraph operators on many of the ships in the area had gone to bed. At that time there was no requirement that a telegraph operator be on duty around the clock. However, even had operators been on duty, few ships were close enough to reach the survivors in time (although there is still disagreement as to the proximity of the *Californian*). The *Carpathia* took about 4.5 hours to arrive on the scene.

❖ Could any ship in the area have reached them sooner?

There is some controversy as to whether the *Californian* was close enough to have rescued all aboard the *Titanic*. The evidence is contradictory. Other than the possibility that the *Californian* might have helped, no other ship was close enough.

❖ Why were there not enough lifeboats for everyone on board?

The British Board of Trade established the rules for the number of lifeboats required based on the gross tonnage of the ship, not the number of people the ship carried. The *Titanic* actually had more lifeboats than required, but only enough for 52% of the people aboard.

❖ Based on how it sank, did ship builders and engineers learn anything new?

Not until the wreck was located was there any definitive information. Even then it was hard to determine what damage was the result of the iceberg (that part of the ship is resting in about 20 feet of sludge at the bottom of the ocean) and what was a result of the breakup. However, comparisons with *Titanic's* sister ship, *Britannic* (sunk by torpedo off the coast of a Greek island during WWI), have definitively provided information about the expansion joint. Interestingly, it appears that the shipbuilder, Harlan & Wolff, realized this possibility within a month of the sinking but kept it a secret so it would not be held liable.

❖ Was the *Titanic* really as strong as the owner said it was?

Not really. The builder simply scaled up a smaller ship and was not certain how the bigger, heavier ship would stress the materials. Some of the design elements of the ship, like its expansion joints, seemed to work on smaller, less heavy ships but were already cracking on the *Olympic* (the first sister ship of the *Titanic*) even before the *Titanic* set sail.

❖ Were any changes made in maritime law and procedure after the accident?

Yes, in 1914 Britain hosted the first SOLAS (Safety of Life at Sea) Conference to craft new safety rules and regulations. The treaty that resulted from this conference has been updated in the years since and is still in force.

- New lifeboat regulations and drills required

- 24-hour radio watch and uniform distress rockets instituted

- International Ice Patrol created

- Ship design changes

- New speed regulations

Now there is enough information to decide which text structure to use for this topic:

TOPIC	TEXT STRUCTURE
What really caused loss of life on the Titanic and how have such catastrophes been avoided since?	Because this topic is really about the chain of events leading up to the sinking and how it helped change maritime regulations, this will be a **cause-effect** paper.

Graphic organizers are simply a bridge to more organized writing. The critical element is to learn how to use them to develop a thesis statement and to determine which of the six expository text structures is the most appropriate for the topic.

Which graphic organizer to use depends on the text structure that most effectively conveys the ideas being discussed. Therefore, when the text structure for a particular topic is initially unclear, the writer may have to first brainstorm as described in the *Topic* section before deciding which graphic organizer to use. Once the appropriate text structure has been determined, or if the structure is clear from the topic, the writer should transfer all collected information to an appropriate analysis organizer (see *Toolbox* section of this guide).

CAUTION: Writers should be aware that simply filling out a graphic organizer will not magically result in the manifestation of a thesis statement. In fact, if a writer is not intentional about developing a thesis statement, she often ends up with an essay that is simply a list taken directly from the graphic organizer.

The following graphic will help to organize the analytical work:

Choosing an Appropriate Graphic Organizer

Select Appropriate Text Structure	Choose Appropriate Graphic Organizer	Develop Thesis Statement	Transfer to Writing Template	Draft, Edit, Final
Compare-Contrast	Compare-Contrast Analysis Organizer Venn Diagram Double Bubble Map	Thesis: Summarize the patterns and relationships between and among the similarities and differences	See writing template & compare-contrast tip sheet	Remember transition language, evidence & editing checklist
Cause-Effect	Cause-Effect Analysis Organizer Multi-Flow Map	Thesis: Summarize the patterns and relationships between and among the causes and effects	See writing template & cause-effect tip sheet	
Concept- Definition	Concept-Definition Analysis Organizer Circle Map (for defining in context) Tree Map (for classifying and grouping) Brace Map (for identifying part/whole relationships)	Thesis: Define the concept and why it is important and summarize the patterns and relationships between and among the information	See writing template & concept-definition tip sheet	

CHOOSING AN APPROPRIATE GRAPHIC ORGANIZER (CONT.)

SELECT APPROPRIATE TEXT STRUCTURE	CHOOSE APPROPRIATE GRAPHIC ORGANIZER	DEVELOP THESIS STATEMENT	TRANSFER TO WRITING TEMPLATE	DRAFT, EDIT, FINAL
Goal-Action-Outcome	Goal-Action-Outcome Analysis Organizer Flow Map	Thesis: Clearly explain goal and (if appropriate) reason for goal	See writing template & goal-action-outcome tip sheet	Remember transition language, evidence & editing checklist
Proposition-Support	Proposition-Support Analysis Organizer Pro/Con Scale	Thesis: Summarize exactly what is believed to be true and why	See writing template & proposition-support tip sheet	
Problem-Solution	Problem-Solution Analysis Organizer	Thesis: Summarize the problem and why it needs to be dealt with	See writing template & problem-solution tip sheet	

Resources for Graphic Organizers

Text Structures Graphic Organizers (Free)
> http://www.cheney268.com/learning/organizers/TextStructures.htm

Thinking Maps   Thinking Maps, Inc.
> http://www.thinkingmaps.com/htthinkmap.php3

Analytic Processes Frameworks   Tregoe Education Forum
> http://www.tregoe.org/work/overview-analytic-process.php

The next page demonstrates a basic multi-flow map (from Thinking Maps, Inc.) completed for the *Titanic* topic:

Causes/Reasons	Event/Situation	Effects/Results
Lookouts didn't have binoculars		Regulations to ensure enough lifeboats for all people aboard and drills in how to use them
Weather calm, clear, no moon, hard to see		24-hour radio watch integrated into the chain of command on board ships
Didn't turn in time		
Angle of impact disastrous	Titanic sinks on maiden voyage, 1,500 people die	Uniform red distress rockets for all ships on the high seas
Engineering failures: Expansion joints Double bottom		International Ice Patrol established in the North Atlantic
Speeding through known ice belt		Ship design changes
Telegraph officers on other ships not on duty 24/7—had gone to bed		Speed regulations when ice present
Not enough lifeboats		
Flares not the right color (no "official" color for distress rockets, but red generally used)		

GETTING STARTED: THE PIECES OF AN ANALYTICAL ESSAY

THESIS STATEMENT: IF NOTHING ELSE, LEARN THIS!

First comes brainstorming and initial research. Next is the **thesis** or **thesis statement**. The thesis statement is the **MOST IMPORTANT ELEMENT OF AN ESSAY**. It is an arguable opinion, based on evidence. Unfortunately, just filling out a graphic organizer will not automatically generate a thesis statement. The writer needs to examine the ideas on the graphic organizer and summarize any relationships or patterns between and among them and explain what they mean in the thesis statement.

The multi-flow map at the end of the last section shows that many of the causes of the *Titanic* catastrophe were common for all ships in the area: calm, clear, dark seas and skies, ice in the area. So why did the *Titanic* hit an iceberg and sink? It looks like human error, and lots of it! Lost binoculars, faulty engineering, telegraph operators off duty, and not enough lifeboats. In summary, the causes of the *Titanic* disaster were multiple human errors.

Now for the effects of the loss of life. No one could bring back the dead, but maritime officials were focused on how they could make transport by sea safer. Official investigative commissions in the U.S. and Britain analyzed what went wrong to make sure it wouldn't happen again. They instituted new rules about the number of lifeboats required, speed limits when sailing through known ice, new rules about telegraph operations, reengineered ships, and standardized distress rockets. To summarize, they improved and standardized safety equipment and procedures.

With that thinking done, here is a possible thesis statement:

> The loss of life on the *Titanic* was due to profound and repeated human error and resulted in improved and standardized emergency equipment and procedures on the high seas.

Someone else might come to a different explanation about why the *Titanic* went down and how such wrecks have since been avoided. But this is this writer's opinion based on his research and questioning. Eventually he will have to "prove" his point, providing evidence from research to logically support this thesis.

The thesis statement is the most critical element of an essay. A writer **MUST** develop the thesis statement before doing anything else because it drives everything that follows. The writer cannot figure out supporting evidence unless she knows what she is supporting!

A thesis statement **CANNOT** be wishy-washy. Pick a side. Odysseus is either a hero or he is not, based on the definition of hero presented in the essay. Do not try to argue both sides. A thesis must be specific.

NOT A THESIS: ~~Odysseus is sometimes a hero and sometimes not.~~ Create "hero" criteria, and then decide whether or not Odysseus fits the criteria. Argue *one* side, not both.

POSSIBLE THESIS: The ancient Greek hero was a morally ambiguous figure who underwent an ordeal in which he struggled against the fear of death. Based on this definition, Odysseus does not qualify as a hero in the Greek sense.

CAUTION: After doing research to support the thesis, a writer might have reason to change his mind. When that happens he needs to revise or change the thesis. That's OK. If the writer no longer believes in the thesis, there is no point in trying to convince others.

The following page extends the basic multi-flow map into a *Cause-Effect Analysis Organizer*, taking into account the need to synthesize information in order to develop a thesis statement. There is an *Analysis Organizer* for each text structure in the *Toolbox* section of this guide.

Causes/Reason	Event/Situation	Effects/Results
Lookouts didn't have binoculars		Regulations to ensure enough lifeboats for all people aboard and drills in how to use them
Weather calm, clear, no moon, hard to see		
Didn't turn in time	Titanic sinks on maiden voyage, 1,500 people die	24-hour radio watch integrated into the chain of command on-board ships
Angle of impact disastrous		
Engineering failures: Expansion joints Double bottom		Uniform distress rockets for all ships on the high seas
Speeding through known ice belt		International Ice Patrol in the North Atlantic
Telegraph officers on other ships not on duty 24/7		Ship design changes
Not enough lifeboats		Speed regulation
Flares not the right color		

Summary: Profound and repeated human error caused the sinking of the *Titanic*.

Summary: The sinking of the *Titanic* resulted in improved and standardized emergency equipment and procedures.

Possible Thesis: The loss of life on the *Titanic* was due to profound and repeated human error and resulted in improved and standardized emergency equipment and procedures on the high seas.

EXAMPLES OF TOPICS & THESIS STATEMENTS FOR EACH TEXT STRUCTURE

TEXT STRUCTURE	TOPIC	SAMPLE THESIS STATEMENT
Compare-Contrast	Compare and contrast the approaches of Malcolm X and Martin Luther King, Jr. to the African-American struggle for civil rights in the 1950s and 60s.	While both Malcolm X and Martin Luther King, Jr. believed that racism and discrimination in the U.S. needed to be eradicated, they held opposing points of view on how to convince white Americans to overcome their long-held beliefs.
Cause-Effect	How did decisions at the end of World War I affect the likelihood of a lasting peace in Europe?	Although the desire for revenge was understandable, the terms of the Treaty of Versailles, as dictated by the Allies, brutally punished Germany after World War I. Unfortunately, these terms lead directly to the rise of the Nazi Party in the 1930s and ultimately the breakout of World War II in 1939.
Problem-Solution	How should healthcare in the United States be reformed?	The healthcare crisis in America has generated many suggestions for reform and a great deal of disagreement; however, one possible solution stands out. Treat healthcare like the necessity it is, with all the rules and regulations required of utilities like electrical, cable, water, and gas companies.

TEXT STRUCTURE	TOPICS	SAMPLE THESIS STATEMENTS
Concept-Definition (descriptive writing)	Does Odysseus fulfill the role of an ancient Greek hero?	Because the traditional ancient Greek hero is a morally ambiguous figure who undergoes an ordeal in which he struggles against the fear of death but ultimately dies, Odysseus does not qualify as a hero in the Greek sense.
Goal-Action-Outcome (process or procedural writing)	Develop a personal fitness plan.	Because fitness and strength are critical when playing contact sports, especially varsity football, this fitness plan will focus on improving cardiovascular endurance and strength and promote better nutrition.
Proposition-Support (persuasive writing)	Is playing video games detrimental to academic achievement?	Contrary to popular belief, playing video games actually enhances positive academic behaviors, honing decision-making/problem-solving skills, persistence, and the understanding of consequences.

Supporting Ideas & Supporting Evidence: What's the Difference?

After establishing her thesis statement, a writer needs to incorporate at least **three supporting ideas** into the essay to prove her point. This is the **Second Most Important Element of an Essay.** Without solid evidence, all that exists is an unsupported opinion, convincing no one. Although every writer should have an opinion (sometimes referred to as an hypothesis), it is not enough to have *only* an opinion.

First, just as patterns and relationships are summarized on a graphic organizer in order to create an effective thesis statement, a writer also has to summarize the evidence gathered in order to generate supporting idea statements. These statements do not provide the actual supporting evidence; they simply summarize it. Always choose the most important or illustrative evidence from the graphic organizer. It is seldom possible or desirable to use all of the evidence gathered.

Begin paragraphs with these supporting idea statements (sometimes referred to as topic sentences) that summarize the point being made. Then elaborate on these summary sentences with specific details and outside evidence in the clearest, most sensible way possible. After summarizing the evidence (supporting idea), the writer must then provide the actual evidence gathered during the research phase (supporting evidence).

First, create topic sentences that summarize the supporting evidence:

CAUSES Example #1
Supporting Idea:
> Captain Smith did not reduce *Titanic's* speed, even though he knew there was ice in the area and many other ships had either stopped for the night or slowed down significantly.

Kinds of Supporting Evidence/Detailed Examples Needed:
> What was the specific chain of events and how did Captain Smith respond at each step? Are there quotes we can use to support our point? Evidence from surviving witnesses?

CAUSES Example #2

Supporting Idea:
> At the time of the collision, no one knew that there were significant problems with the strength of the expansion joints.

Kinds of Supporting Evidence/Detailed Examples Needed:
> Explain in detail what an expansion joint is. Why was it important in this case? Why didn't the engineers know better?

CAUSES Example #3

Supporting Idea:
> Once the Captain realized the ship was mortally wounded, he instituted emergency procedures: SOS telegraphs and distress rockets, but they were ultimately unsuccessful.

Kinds of Supporting Evidence/Detailed Examples Needed:
> Explain in detail how these procedures did not result in rescue. Look for quotes and evidence from survivors.

CAUSES Example #4

Supporting Idea:

The last option for saving people's lives was to put them in life-boats. Had there been enough lifeboats to hold everyone, this might have worked.

Kinds of Supporting Evidence/Detailed Examples Needed:

Explain why there were not enough lifeboats. What were the regulations at the time? Was the White Star Line negligent? Why or why not?

EFFECTS Example #1

Supporting Idea:

The International Ice Patrol (IIP) was established and new rules agreed upon concerning how ships should deal with ice.

Kinds of Supporting Evidence/Detailed Examples Needed:

What is the IIP? What were the specific rules put in place? How have they helped make shipping safer? Show statistics.

EFFECTS Example #2

Supporting Idea:

The expansion joints of large ships were redesigned. The first expansion joints to be retrofitted were those of the *Britannic*, *Titanic's* sister ship.

Kinds of Supporting Evidence/Detailed Examples Needed:

When/how did this come to light? What were the redesigns?

<u>EFFECTS Example #3</u>

Supporting Idea:

After the sinking, new emergency communications regulations were put into effect.

Kinds of Supporting Evidence/Detailed Examples Needed:

What were they specifically? Explain.

<u>EFFECTS Example #4</u>

Supporting Idea:

The most recognizable change after the sinking was the new international requirement that there be enough lifeboats to evacuate all people aboard and that passengers and crew be drilled in how to use them.

Kinds of Supporting Evidence/Detailed Examples Needed:

Explain the specifics of the change. What are the effects today?

Once the topic sentences summarizing the supporting ideas are in place, then the writer can focus on organizing the evidence, collecting the details and explanations necessary to verify the assertions. Supporting evidence can be any or all of the following, depending on what is appropriate for the topic:

- ❖ Someone else's research;

- ❖ Data—graphs, charts, tables, etc.;

- ❖ Logically argued opinions of reliable experts;

- ❖ Personal accounts of eye-witnesses;

- ❖ Similar current or historical events;

- ❖ Mathematical proofs; and/or

❖ Quotes from a text

In the case of the *Titanic* example, we have found the following evidence to support our topic sentences.

CAUSES Example #1

Supporting Idea:

Captain Smith knew there was ice in the area and many other ships had either stopped for the night or slowed down significantly.

Specific Supporting Evidence/Detailed Example:

Had the telegraph officers passed on *all* the ice warnings, it would have been clear to the officers that there was "a huge field of ice some 78 miles long directly ahead of the *Titanic*." (*Titanic*. p. 20) Captain Smith knew of the existence of some ice because he had discussed it with the ship's owner, Bruce Ismay, in front of passengers earlier in the day. (*Titanic*, pp. 17-18)

Although "it was customary, at that time, for ships to travel at full speed until a berg was actually sighted...." (Titanic p. 19) many other ships in the area had slowed significantly or, in the case of the ship closest to the *Titanic*, the *Californian*, stopped for the night.

Supporting Idea:

At the time of the collision, no one knew that there were significant problems with the strength of the expansion joints.

Specific Supporting Evidence/Detailed Example:

Expansion joints are slight gaps in the upper hull of a large ship that allow it to "flex" as it travels through waves and troughs. Andrews, the ship's designer, "knew that the hull girder would have to be strong enough to span the crests of two or more waves, flex at the ends, and twist in several directions at the same time—but not break." (Secrets, p. 99)

The ship designers had "no idea whether *Olympic* and *Titanic* were strong enough to hold together at sea.... [they] simply scaled up the hull of *Oceanic* and smaller ships...." (Secrets, pp. 237-38) The result was a flawed ocean liner. Research has shown that "the expansion joint under the third funnel was a critically weak point in the ship." (Secrets, p. 246)

Had the expansion joints been stronger or had the ship been engineered differently altogether, the *Titanic* would have floated for many more hours, allowing other ships to come to the rescue. As the incoming water weighed down the center of the ship, the expansion joints failed catastrophically, folding in on themselves, and causing the ship to quickly break apart. "The laws of strength and buoyancy that had inspired [Andrews] his entire life doomed *Titanic*. Thousands of tons of seawater would quickly outweigh the ability of the ship's hull to support it." (Secrets, 166)

Supporting Idea:

Once the Captain realized the ship was mortally wounded, he instituted emergency procedures: SOS telegraphs and distress rockets, but they were ultimately unsuccessful.

Specific Supporting Evidence/Detailed Example:

Ships' telegraph officers were employed by the Marconi Company, were not part of the official chain of command on board ship, and did not work 24/7. "The Marconi wireless radio operators, were...paid to relay messages to and from the passengers, they were not focused on relaying such "non-essential" ice messages to the bridge." (Ballard's Titanic, p. 20) The telegraph officer on the *Californian*, the closest ship to the *Titanic*, had gone to bed only five minutes before *Titanic* sent her first distress call.

Captain Smith also ordered the crew to start firing distress rockets. At that time many ships still used signal flares and there was no standardized color for distress rockets. Though most seamen recognized red flares to mean distress, the *Titanic* had only white rockets. These were mistaken by the *Californian* to be either celebratory or communications flares.

CAUSES Example #4

Supporting Idea:

The last option for saving people's lives was to put them in lifeboats. Had there been enough lifeboats to hold everyone, this might have worked.

Specific Supporting Evidence/Detailed Example:

The British Board of Trade required only that "any ship over 10,000 tons...had to carry sixteen lifeboats [approximately 960 people—the *Titanic* carried 2200 passengers and crew]...." (Secrets, p. 101) This regulation was dependant on the tonnage of the ship, not the number of people it carried. When she sailed the "*Titanic* actually carried *more* lifeboats than the [regulations] required." (Titanic, p. 22)

Titanic had 20 lifeboats of three different types:
Lifeboats 1 and 2: emergency wooden cutters (40 persons each)
Lifeboats 3 to 16: wooden lifeboats (65 persons each)
Lifeboats A, B, C, and D: Englehardt "collapsible" lifeboats (47 persons each)
"Titanic's life saving appliances". *British Wreck Commissioner's Inquiry.* 1912-07-30.

On the *Titanic* Harland & Wolff had included the new Welin lifeboat davits (crane-like devices used to raise and lower lifeboats). So the ship could have carried on board up to 48 lifeboats, enough for 2880 people. However, when it came time to provision the boat, Ismay decided 16 wooden lifeboats and four collapsible boats would be enough boats to "ferry passengers to a rescue ship. The [*Titanic*] should surely be able stay afloat long enough for help to arrive.... Why clutter the boat deck promenade with three dozen more boats than the law required?" (Secrets, p. 104) Thus, even if the existing lifeboats had been filled to capacity before they were launched, over 1,000 people still would have died.

Supporting Idea:

(Transition from causes to effects) "*The sheer dimensions of the Titanic disaster created sufficient public reaction on both sides of the Atlantic to prod reluctant governments into action, producing the first Safety of Life at Sea (SOLAS) convention in 1914.*" The purpose of the SOLAS treaty was to "ensure that in the event of a catastrophe at sea passengers and crew have the greatest chance of survival." (IIP web site)

The first order of business of SOLAS was to establish the International Ice Patrol (IIP) and agree to new rules concerning how ships would cope with ice.

Specific Supporting Evidence/Detailed Example:

The IIP began the air reconnaissance of the shipping lanes in the North Atlantic that continues today. Its role is to investigate and then communicate ice conditions. In addition, when ice is reported by the IIP, ships are required to "proceed at moderate speed or alter course." (IIP web site).

EFFECTS Example #2

Supporting Idea:

The expansion joints of large ships were redesigned. The retrofitted expansion joints and steel reinforcement on the *Britannic* was completed after *Titanic* sank.

Specific Supporting Evidence/Detailed Example:

During the summer of 2006, divers explored the *Britannic* where it rests on the bottom of the Aegean Sea. They confirmed that Harland & Wolff had significantly changed the expansion joint design on *Britannic*.

That the company didn't announce this fact to the world is testament to its fear of being sued by the families of the victims of the *Titanic* disaster. The ship's designers and builders decided on their own to "build *Britannic* with a double hull, and redesign the expansion joint and other weak points in the ships. There was no law that required them to do that. *Titanic* had perfectly conformed to the regulations of the British Board of Trade." (Secrets, p. 241)

EFFECTS Example #3

Supporting Idea:

Also at the SOLAS convention, new maritime communications regulations were put into effect.

Specific Supporting Evidence/Detailed Example:

Ships were required to have a telegraph operator on duty around the clock who reported directly to the Captain. Also required were red rockets to be used only in cases of distress and which "must be interpreted as a distress signal" by all ships in sight. (IIP web site)

EFFECTS Example #4

Supporting Idea:

The most recognizable change after the sinking was the significant new lifeboat requirements, which were specifically crafted to respond to those aspects of the *Titanic* disaster that resulted in unnecessary injury and death.

Specific Supporting Evidence/Detailed Example:

The most visible change after the *Titanic* disaster was the new the SOLAS regulation that required that all ships, passenger and cargo, have enough lifeboats for all "souls" on board, plus rafts for an additional 25%. In addition, all ships must have a public address system. *Titanic* did not have one, so most of the passengers had no idea what was happening as the ship went down.

On the *Titanic*, there had been no emergency drills upon sailing. Neither had the crew been properly trained to load and lower full lifeboats and no one knew which lifeboat he had been assigned to. SOLAS now requires that "Abandon Ship" and "Fire Onboard" drills must take place weekly on passenger ships and that there be regular and ongoing crew training.

Evacuation chutes like those used on airplanes were developed and are now required to assist in the loading of the lifeboats.

Many *Titanic* passengers died of hypothermia and exposure, especially those who had become wet for one reason or another. As a result, SOLAS requires that the lifeboats on ships that sail the North Atlantic must be enclosed in order to protect survivors from the cold and weather. (IIP web site)

Write as many paragraphs as needed to prove the point being made in the thesis.

The general rule of thumb is that a writer needs *at least* three solid supporting ideas to make a convincing argument, so there should be at least three body paragraphs. Because it takes three of anything to indicate a pattern, any fewer than three strong supporting ideas means the thesis is weak and lacks support. However, it may take more than a paragraph to fully explain each piece of supporting evidence. If that is the case, take all the space needed.

Many people in a variety of professions use this rule. For example, journalists need three credible sources to confirm a story before they can print it; otherwise they can be sued for libel. Scientists must replicate an experiment with the same exact results three times before the scientific community will accept the conclusions as valid. Lawyers follow this rule when arguing cases in front of a judge, as do preachers when composing sermons.

REMEMBER: A writer needs at least three relevant ideas to support a thesis. Each individual paragraph (or group of related paragraphs) should focus on one of these. Do not mix up the ideas; it confuses the reader.

Now that we have a thesis and (at least) three supporting ideas, it's time to summarize for the reader what those ideas are. The **statement of structure** tells the reader the general nature of the supporting ideas that will be addressed in detail in the body of the essay as well as the order in which they will be introduced.

The body of the essay goes into more detail, of course, but a writer needs to provide the reader with a map of the journey. In the *Titanic* example, the statement of structure is underline:

> The loss of life on the *Titanic* was due to <u>profound and repeated human error</u> and resulted in improved and <u>standardized emergency equipment and procedures</u> on the high seas.

In this case the statement of structure is implied; that is, it is dealt with within the thesis statement. A statement of structure can be implicit or explicit. An **implicit** statement of structure is communicated within the thesis statement. In the *Titanic* example, the reader knows the first examples in the body of the essay will address the human error and then the essay will outline the new safety regulations.

This is another example of an implicit statement of structure:

> Every school can do more to <u>reduce, reuse, and recycle</u> resources to decrease its carbon footprint. (proposition-support)

This implied statement of structure indicates that the reader will first read about how to reduce waste, then what we can reuse, and finally what we can recycle. The order in which the ideas appear in the statement of structure—whether within or outside of the thesis statement—should be the order in which the writer addresses them in the essay.

At other times, the statement of structure can be explicit. It is a separate sentence that comes after the thesis statement and explains how the paper will be structured:

When friends are mean to each other it is called Relational Aggression. The reasons for Relational Aggression are varied but include <u>jealousy, anger, and the need for control</u>. (concept-definition)

Always try for an implicit statement of structure: it is a hallmark of concise thinking and writing. However, first draft thesis statements often employ explicit statements of structure so the writer does not forget to address the supporting arguments. As the essay is reworked, moving towards the final draft, often an explicit statement of structure is replaced by an implicit statement of structure.

Although it may appear to be redundant, the statement of structure is necessary. It keeps both the writer and the reader focused on the argument. Be sure to include it!

Next comes the **lead-in** (sometimes referred to as the **hook**). While the thesis statement is specific to the topic being addressed, the lead-in provides broader context, explaining why the reader should care about the thesis. Using the *Titanic* example, the lead-in might look like this:

Lead-in: Any time an accident results in significant loss of life, people demand to know why such a tragedy occurred and whether or not it could have been avoided. Today, the Nation Transportation Safety Board (NTSB) conducts an investigation each time a plane, ship, or train is involved in such a disaster. The tragedy that started it all was the sinking of the *RMS Titanic*. On her maiden voyage, just before midnight on April 14, 1912, the *Titanic* hit an iceberg and sunk in an astonishingly quick two hours and 23 minutes, killing 1,500 people. It remains the worst maritime disaster of all time. In its aftermath everyone demanded answers.

Followed by the…

Thesis: Although the loss of life on the *Titanic* was due to profound and repeated human error, it resulted in improved and standardized emergency equipment and procedures on the high seas.

Providing a wider social context for the very specific *Titanic* thesis statement helps readers understand why they might want to read the essay. The lead-in needs to answer the question, "Why should the audience care?" When constructing a lead-in, it helps to reflect on why a teacher has assigned the topic. What big idea is the teacher trying to help students understand? What general lessons can be learned from it? Why is this topic important in the real world? How might it relate to something else previously studied?

Notes

Readers understand the thinking behind an essay by following the language that links ideas in a logical way. It is precise **transition words/phrases** that effectively lead a reader through an argument. Words and phrases like:

however	because	purpose is	in spite of
either/or	therefore	finally	unfortunately
nevertheless	consequently	opinions include	fortunately
although	so that	topic is	just as
both	in order to	belief	in contrast to
as well as	the cause is	idea	similarly
not only	results are	in preference to	hereby
but also	analysis shows	hypotheses	while
as a result	steps taken	theory	ironically
since	effects are	one might assume	amazingly
this led to	similar viewpoint	on the other hand	disturbingly
if ....then	alternative viewpoint	before	first, second, etc.
whereby		after	next

A writer wants a reader to follow his train of thought exactly. Transition words and phrases are like the nubs and slots on a puzzle piece. The piece (or idea) needs to fit perfectly into the one next to it in order for the whole puzzle to work. Learning sentence (idea) combining is one way students grasp how to incorporate transition language effectively. It is such an important component of expository writing that the first supplement to this guide deals solely with sentence (idea) combining.

At last and finally comes the conclusion. What exactly is a conclusion? The conclusion ties up loose ends; **no new information or ideas should come into the conclusion!!**

Now that the reader has assimilated the evidence provided, the writer wants to remind her once more what he was trying to prove and why it is important. A restatement of the thesis statement related to the broader world must be part of the conclusion (remember that lead-in; it will be revisited here). However, if the author has not clearly explained his thesis, it is impossible to write an appropriate conclusion.

There are three parts to a concluding paragraph:

- ❖ Restatement of the thesis (using different words or different point of view):
- ❖ Summary of the main points (using different words or different point of view):
- ❖ Universal applications (return to the lead-in in the introductory paragraph and echo those ideas, but using different words):

In the *Titanic* essay, the conclusion might look like this:

Restatement of thesis (using different words or different point of view):

While all would have preferred the *Titanic* passengers and crew who died to have enjoyed long lives, the shipping industry did learn a great deal from the multiple errors and miscalculations that lead to the appalling loss of life.

Recap of main points (using different words or different point of view):

In the wake of the calamity, new safety regulations went into effect, the International Ice Patrol (IIP) was established to provide information and track ice in the North Atlantic, new communications regulations were instituted, and ships are required to carry enough lifeboats for all onboard and to drill passengers in how to use them.

Universal applications (return to the lead-in in the introductory paragraph and echo those ideas—using different words):

Without the analysis precipitated by the *Titanic* catastrophe, the shipping industry would not have had the information it needed to make informed decisions about what improvements to implement. The safety legacy of the *Titanic* exists to this day in the form of the lifeboat drills passengers participate in every time they begin a cruise. So when complaining because the lifeboat drill interrupts a dip in the ship's pool, remember the alternative!

Ways to wrap up a conclusion:

❖ An emotional appeal based on supporting facts. This was used above.

❖ A call to action

❖ A pertinent quotation

❖ A provocative question related to the topic

REMEMBER: No new ideas or information appear in a conclusion.

When a piece of writing is long enough to merit a title, it should reflect the central theme or idea of the essay. The best titles rely on word-play, pithy puns, and double meanings.

In general, don't waste too much time thinking up a title; it is far better to have a great essay and a mundane title than the other way around. However, for big projects it's worth spending some time concentrating on it. So what about a title for the sample essay?

Over time, the word "titanic" has morphed into an adjective that means enormous and God-like. It comes from Greek mythology. The Titans were the fathers and mothers of the Olympian gods. So the word can be used both as the name *Titanic* and as an adjective describing something enormous in size and/or powerful in concept.

The essay focuses on the significant human errors—mistakes—that caused the loss of life.

So, our title will be *Titanic* Mistakes.

This title uses the word "titanic" to indicate both the ship's mistakes and their huge significance.

BONUS: Explain the word play used in the title of this book!

THE MANY PIECES BECOME A WHOLE

ASSEMBLING THE PIECES OF THE PUZZLE

BIG PICTURE	PART OF THE ESSAY	PURPOSE OF THE PART
	Introduction	
Inform readers what the essay is about.	Lead-in	Sets context for the piece—why is this idea important in terms of the big picture?
	Thesis Statement	Explicitly tells the reader what the argument is about.
	Statement of Structure	Explicitly tells the reader the elements of the argument.
	Supporting Idea I	
Provide readers with: • Logical reasoning • Credible external evidence • Factual examples • References where appropriate	Summary Sentence	Introduces and summarizes Idea # One.
	Evidence	Provides explanation and evidence for Idea # One only.
	Supporting Idea II	
	Summary Sentence	Introduces and summarizesIdea # Two.
	Evidence	Provides explanation and evidence for Idea # Two only.
	Supporting Idea III	
	Summary Sentence	Introduces and summarizes Idea # Three.
	Evidence	Provides explanation and evidence for Idea # Three only.
	Conclusion: NEVER INTRODUCE NEW INFORMATION IN THE CONCLUSION!	
Remind readers what the essay is all about.	Restatement of thesis	Summarizes thesis using different words or point of view than in the introduction.
	Recap of main points	Briefly summarizesthe(at least) three pieces of evidence.
	Universal application	Reminds reader of the context the set at the beginning of the essay.

Notes

The First Draft: Plain Hard Work

The first time the writer links all the related ideas together is in the first draft. It can be overwhelming. Think of it as beginning that 5,000-piece puzzle; it is a bit daunting, but by developing a strategy and working slowly and steadily the essay will start to take shape.

Remember to pay attention to the following:

- ❖ Write a clear, focused, defendable thesis;

- ❖ Construct a logical argument that includes a statement of structure and transition language;

- ❖ Explain/identify all critical terms and people;

- ❖ Include at least one appropriate example, preferably more, per supporting idea—scientific evidence, historical examples and/or quotations, a mathematical expression; and

- ❖ Use linguistic cues to keep the reader on track, especially transitional ideas and phrases, plus subtle repetition of key terms.

Activity: Compare the notes made while organizing the information in the *Supporting Ideas* section with this first draft. Highlight and then explain why new material was added.

Titanic Mistakes

Any time an accident results in significant loss of life, people demand to know how such a tragedy occurred and whether or not it could have been avoided. In fact, today the Nation Transportation Safety Board (NTSB) conducts such investigations each time a plane, ship, or train is involved in such an accident. The tragedy that started it all was the sinking of the *RMS Titanic.* Just before midnight on April 14, 1912, the Titanic hit an iceberg on her maiden voyage and sunk in an astonishingly quick two hours and twenty-three minutes, killing 1500 people. It was, and remains, the worst maritime disaster of all time. In its aftermath everyone demanded answers. Although the loss of life on the Titanic was due to profound and repeated human error, it precipitated in improved and standardized emergency equipment and procedures on the high seas.

It is not true that on the evening of April 14 Captain Smith sped up to prove a point about the ship. However, he did not reduce *Titanic's* speed, even though he knew there was ice in the area and many other ships had either stopped for the night or slowed down significantly. Had the telegraph officers passed on all the ice warnings, it would have been clear to the officers that there was "a huge field of ice some 78 miles long directly ahead of the *Titanic*." (*Titanic.* p. 20) However, we know that Captain Smith knew of the existence of some ice because he had discussed it with the ship's owner, Bruce Ismay, in front of passengers earlier in the day. (*Titanic,* pp. 17-18) Although "it was customary, at that time, for ships to travel at full speed until a berg was actually sighted...." (Titanic p. 19), many other ships in the area had slowed significantly or, in the case of the ship closest to the *Titanic,* the *Californian,* stopped for the night.

At the time of the collision, no one knew that there were significant problems with the strength of the expansion joints. Expansion joints are slight gaps in the upper hull of a large ship that allow the ship to "flex" as it travels through waves and troughs. Thomas Andrews, the ship's designer, "knew that the hull girder would have to be strong enough to span the crests of two or more waves, flex at the ends, and twist in several directions at the same time—but not break." (Secrets, p. 99) The ship designers had "no idea whether *Olympic* and *Titanic* were strong enough to hold together at sea.... [they] simply scaled up the hull of *Oceanic* and smaller ships...." (Secrets, p. 237-38) In so doing, they ended up with a flawed ocean liner. Subsequent research has shown "the expansion joint under the third funnel was a critically weak point in the ship." (Secrets, p. 246)

Had the expansion joints been stronger or had the ship been engineered differently altogether, it is likely that *Titanic* would have floated for many more hours, allowing other ships to come to the rescue. In reality, as the incoming water weighed down the center of the ship, the expansion joints failed catastrophically, folding in on themselves, and causing the ship to quickly break apart. "The laws of strength and buoyancy that had inspired [Andrews] his entire life doomed *Titanic*. Thousands of tons of seawater would quickly outweigh the ability of the ships hull to support it" (Secrets, 166).

Once the Captain realized the ship was mortally wounded, he instituted emergency procedures: SOS telegraphs and distress rockets, but they were ultimately unsuccessful. Before the *Titanic* sank, ships' telegraph officers worked for the Marconi Company, were not part of the official chain of command onboard ship, and did not work around the clock. In fact, "the Marconi wireless radio operators were...paid to relay messages to and from the passengers, they were not focused on relaying such 'non-essential' ice messages to the bridge." (Titanic, p. 20) As a result of this non-official role, the telegraph officer on the *Californian*, the closest ship to the *Titanic*, was not awake and working; he had gone to bed only five minutes before *Titanic* sent her first distress call.

As a last resort, Captain Smith ordered the crew to start firing distress rockets. At that time many ships still used signal flares in general, which had been the way to communicate from ship to ship before the telegraph. As a result, there was no standardized color for the distress rockets. Most people recognized red flares to mean distress, but the *Titanic* only had white rockets. These were mistaken as either celebratory or communications flares by the *Californian*.

The last option for saving people's lives was to put them in lifeboats. Had there been enough lifeboats to hold everyone, this might have worked. However, prior to *Titanic* tragedy the British Board of Trade required only that "any ship over 10,000 tons...had to carry sixteen lifeboats [approximately 960 people—the *Titanic* carried 2,200 passengers and crew]...." (Secrets, p. 101) This regulation was dependant on the tonnage of the ship, not the number of people it carried. Ironically, when she sailed the "*Titanic* actually carried *more* lifeboats than the [regulations] required." (Titanic, p. 22)

Available to *Titanic's* passengers and crew were 20 lifeboats of three different varieties:

❖ Lifeboats 1 and 2: emergency wooden cutters (40 persons each)
❖ Lifeboats 3 to 16: wooden lifeboats (65 persons each)
❖ Lifeboats A, B, C, and D: Englehardt "collapsible" lifeboats (47 persons each)

("Titanic's life saving appliances". *British Wreck Commissioner's Inquiry.* 1912-07-30.)

So, for the approximately 2,220 passengers and crew, there were lifeboat seats for 1,178, *if* all boats had left the ship full, which they did not. In the end, only approximately 700 people survived.

Interestingly, because they anticipated a future change in lifeboat regulations, Harland & Wolff had included the new Welin lifeboats davits (crane-like devices used to raise and lower lifeboats) on the *Titanic*. As a result, she could have carried up to 48 lifeboats onboard [for 2,880 people]. However, when it came time to make the decision to provision the boat, Ismay decided on 16 wooden lifeboats and four collapsible boats. Ismay felt that this would be plenty of boats to "ferry passengers to a rescue ship. The [*Titanic*] should surely be able stay afloat long enough for help to arrive.... Why clutter the boat deck promenade with three dozen more boats than the law required?" (Secrets, p. 104) So even if the lifeboats had all been filled before launch, over 1,000 people would still have perished that April night in 1912.

"The sheer dimensions of the *Titanic* disaster created sufficient public reaction on both sides of the Atlantic to prod reluctant governments into action, producing the first Safety of Life at Sea (SOLAS) convention in 1914" (IIP web site). The purpose of the SOLAS treaty, which has been continuously updated since 1914, is to "ensure that in the event of a catastrophe at sea, passengers and crew have the greatest chance of survival" (IIP web site). The first order of business of SOLAS was to found the International Ice Patrol (IIP) and agree to new rules about how ships were to deal with ice.

Within a few weeks after *Titanic* sank, the IIP began the air reconnaissance of the ice lanes in the North Atlantic that continues today. Their role is to investigate and communicate the ice conditions in the shipping lanes of the North Atlantic. In addition, when ice is reported by the IIP, ships are required to "proceed at moderate speed or alter course" (IIP web site).

The expansion joints of large ships were redesigned, as evidenced by the retrofitted expansion joints and steel reinforcement on the *Britannic*, *Titanic's* sister ship, completed after she sank. During the summer of 2006, divers were able to dive the 400 feet to where *Britannic* rests on the bottom of the Aegean Sea, after running into a mine during World War I. Sure enough, they discovered evidence that Harland & Wolff had significantly changed the expansion joint design on *Britannic*.

That the company didn't announce it to the world is testament to their fear of being sued by the families of the victims of the *Titanic* disaster. Secretly, quietly, without fanfare, the ship's designers and builders decided on their own to "build *Britannic* with a double hull, and redesign the expansion joint and other weak points in the ships. There was no law that required them to do that. *Titanic* had perfectly conformed to the regulations of the British Board of

Trade." (Secrets, p. 241)

Also at SOLAS, new maritime communications regulations were put into effect. After the *Titanic* sank it was required that ships have an around the clock telegraph operator who reported directly to the Captain, as well as red rockets that were only to be used only in cases of distress and "must be interpreted as a distress signal" by all ships in sight. (reference?)

The most recognizable change after the sinking was the significant new lifeboat requirements, which were specifically crafted to respond to those aspects of the *Titanic* disaster that resulted in unnecessary injury and death. The simplest change after the *Titanic* disaster was the new requirement that all ships have a public address system. Amazingly, *Titanic* did not have one, so most of the passengers were in the dark as to what was happening as the ship went down.

As a result of the *Titanic's* lifeboats being insufficient to evacuate all aboard, the SOLAS regulations now require that all ships, passenger and cargo, have enough lifeboats for all "souls" on board, plus rafts for an additional 25 percent. The additional life rafts can be used if all the lifeboats have left the ship minimally loaded and there are still people on board.

Everyone was so complacent about *Titanic's* "unsinkability" that there had been no emergency drills upon sailing. Neither had the crew been properly trained to load and lower full lifeboats and no one knew to which lifeboats they had been assigned. As a result, SOLAS now requires that "Abandon Ship" and "Fire Onboard" drills must take place weekly on passenger ships and that there be regular and ongoing crew training. (IIP web site)

In order to avoid some of the injuries that occurred as passengers from *Titanic* tried to jump into moving lifeboats, evacuation chutes like those used on airplanes were developed and are now used to assist in the loading of the lifeboats.

And finally, of those *Titanic* passengers who did make it to the lifeboats, many died of hypothermia and exposure, especially those who had become wet for one reason or another. As a result, the SOLAS Treaty now requires that the lifeboats on ships that sail the North Atlantic must be able to be enclosed for protection from the cold and weather. (IIP web site)

While all would have preferred the *Titanic* and her passengers and crew to have had long lives, the shipping industry did learn a great deal from the multiple errors and miscalculations that lead to the appalling loss of life. In the wake of the disaster, new safety regulations were put into effect, the International Ice Patrol was founded to provide information about and track ice in the North Atlantic, new communications regulations were instituted, and all ships are now required to carry enough lifeboats for all on board and to drill passengers in how to use them. Without the analysis that went on after the *Titanic* catastrophe, the shipping industry would not have had the information needed to make informed decisions about what safety improvements to implement to prevent a repeat disaster. The safety legacy of the *Titanic* is still with us in the form of the lifeboat drills we participate in every time we begin a cruise. So next time you are on a cruise and the lifeboat drill interrupts a dip in the pool, remember the alternative.

Words: 1989

Now that the pieces have been put together and transition words added, the essay is almost finished. Usually, the first draft is adequate, but the final draft needs to be concise. The idea is to eliminate any overly repetitive or clumsy language.

Continue to check for the following:
- ❖ A clear, focused, defendable thesis;

- ❖ A logically constructed argument that includes a statement of structure and transition language;

- ❖ All critical terms and people explained/identified;

- ❖ Numerous examples, mathematical expressions, scientific evidence, historical examples and/or quotations per supporting idea; and

- ❖ Linguistic cues to keep the reader on track, especially transitional ideas and phrases, and subtle repetition of key terms.

Also, don't forget to use the following editing checklist (found in the *Toolbox* section of this book):
- ❖ Remove slang, contractions, "text" spelling, and abbreviations.

- ❖ Remove first or second person (*I* or *you*) references.

- ❖ Ensure that quotes and evidence are introduced, explained, and integrated, not just dropped in randomly.

- ❖ Make sure quoted, paraphrased, and factual information is appropriately referenced using the relevant format. This is most often the MLA format, but check with the person who assigned the task.

- ❖ Clearly show the relationship between and among ideas using appropriate and varied transition words and phrases.

- ❖ Use accurate punctuation to show the relationship between and among ideas.

- ❖ Replace imprecise words with precise vocabulary. Eliminate *thing*, *stuff*, *very*, *always*, *never*, *sort of*, *a lot*, etc. Replace them with the appropriate, specific words.

- ❖ Confirm verb tenses are consistent within the timeframe(s) being addressed.

- ❖ Mare sure that all singular and plural subjects agree with their verbs.

- ❖ Spell all words correctly: (specifically *their*, *there*, and *they're*; *to*, *too*, and *two*; *and it and it's*).

- ❖ Make sure the title communicates the thesis.

ACTIVITY: Compare the first draft of the *Titanic* essay with this final draft. Highlight what has been added or deleted and explain why this occurred.

Titanic Mistakes

Any time an accident results in a significant loss of life, people demand to know how such a tragedy could have occurred and whether or not it could have been avoided. In fact, the Nation Transportation Safety Board conducts an investigation each time a plane, ship, or train is involved in such an accident. Just before midnight on April 14, 1912, midway through her maiden voyage, the passenger liner *RMS Titanic* hit an iceberg and sunk in an astonishingly quick two hours and 23 minutes, killing 1,500 people. It was, and remains, the worst maritime disaster of all time. In its aftermath everyone demanded answers. Although the loss of life on the *Titanic* was due to profound and repeated human error, it did precipitate improved and standardized emergency equipment and procedures used on the high seas even today.

It is not true that on that fateful Sunday evening, Captain Smith had increased *Titanic's* speed in order to try to break a speed record. However, it is true that he did not reduce *Titanic's* speed, even though he knew there was ice in the area and many other ships had either stopped for the night or slowed down significantly. Had the ship's telegraph operators passed on *all* the ice warnings, it would have been clear to the captain that there was "a huge field of ice some 78 miles long directly ahead of the *Titanic*" (Ballard 20). However, Captain Smith did know of the existence of some ice because he had discussed it with the ship's owner, Bruce Ismay, in front of passengers earlier in the day (*Titanic* 17-18). Although "it was customary, at that time, for ships to travel at full speed until a berg was actually sighted..." (Ballard 19), many other ships in the area had slowed significantly or, in the case of the ship closest to the *Titanic*, the *Californian*, stopped for the night.

Because it was hidden from view at the time of the collision, no one knew there were significant problems with the strength of the ship's expansion joints. These expansion joints are the slight gaps in the upper hull of a large ship that allow it to flex as it travels through waves and troughs. Thomas Andrews, the *Titanic's* designer, "knew that the hull girder would have to be strong enough to span the crests of two or more waves, flex at the ends, and twist in several directions at the same time—but not break" (Matsen 99). However, Andrews had "no idea whether *Olympic* [*Titanic's* sister ship, built before *Titanic*] and *Titanic* were strong enough to hold together at sea.... [he] simply scaled up the hull of *Oceanic* and smaller ships..." (Matsen 237-38). In so doing, he ended up with a flawed ocean liner. Subsequent research has shown that "the expansion joint under the third funnel was a critically weak point in the ship" (Matsen p. 246).

Had the expansion joints been stronger or had the ship been engineered differently altogether, it is likely that *Titanic* would have floated for many more hours, allowing other ships to come to the rescue. In reality, as the incoming water weighed down the center of the ship, the expansion joints failed catastrophically, folding in on themselves and causing the ship to quickly break apart. "The laws of strength and buoyancy that had inspired [Andrews] his entire life doomed *Titanic*. Thousands of tons of seawater would quickly outweigh the ability of the ship's hull to support it" (Matsen 166).

Once Captain Smith realized the ship was mortally wounded, he instituted emergency communications: SOS telegraphs and distress rockets, but they were ultimately unsuccessful. Before the *Titanic* sank, telegraph officers on all ships were employed by the Marconi Company, were not part of the official chain of command aboard ship, and did not work around the clock. In fact, "the Marconi wireless radio operators, were...paid to relay messages to and from the passengers, they were not focused on relaying such 'non-essential' ice messages to the bridge" (Ballard 20). As a result of this non-official role, the telegraph officer on the *Californian*, the closest ship to the *Titanic*, was not awake and on duty; he had gone to bed only five minutes before *Titanic* sent her first distress call. Even the telegraph operator on the *Carpathia*, the ship that eventually rescued *Titanic's* survivors, had been undressing for bed and randomly listening to the telegraph traffic when he heard *Titanic's* distress call. Five more minutes and the telegraph would have been turned off (Ballard 20).

As a last resort at communicating their plight to nearby ships, Captain Smith ordered the crew to fire distress rockets. At that time many ships still occasionally used signal flares, because it had been the only way to communicate from ship to ship before the invention of the telegraph just years before. "All sorts of rockets and flares were used in 1912, procedures covering distress signals at sea were in a state of flux, and some company signals were white" (Ballard 199). Unfortunately, at that time there was no standardized color for distress rockets. Though most seamen recognized red flares to mean distress, the *Titanic* had only white rockets. These were mistaken by the *Californian* to be either celebratory fireworks or company signals.

The last option for saving the passengers' lives was to put them in lifeboats. Had there been enough boats to hold everyone, this might have worked. However, prior to the *Titanic* tragedy the British Board of Trade required only that "any ship over 10,000 tons...had to carry sixteen lifeboats" [approximately 960 people—the *Titanic* carried 2,200 passengers and crew]... (Matsen 101). This regulation was dependant on the tonnage of the ship, not the number of people it carried. Ironically, when she sailed, the "*Titanic* actually carried *more* lifeboats than the [regulations] required." (Ballard 22)

Available to rescue *Titanic's* passengers and crew that April night were 20 lifeboats of three different types:

❖ Lifeboats 1 and 2: emergency wooden cutters (40 persons each)
❖ Lifeboats 3 to 16: wooden lifeboats (65 persons each)
❖ Lifeboats A, B, C, and D: Englehardt "collapsible" lifeboats (47 persons each)
(British Inquiry, http://www.titanicinquiry.org/about.php; 5-April-2010)

For the approximately 2,220 passengers and crew on board that night, there were lifeboat seats for 1,178, *if* all boats had left the ship full, which they did not (Ballard 22). In the end, only 705 people survived (Winocour 9).

Interestingly, because Harland & Wolff, the company that built *Titanic*, had anticipated a future change in lifeboat regulations, it had installed on the ship the newly developed Welin lifeboat davits (crane-like devices used to raise and lower lifeboats) that enable multiple boats to be lowered from the same davit. As a result, she could have carried up to 48 lifeboats on board, enough to save 2,880 people. However, when it came time to make the decision to provision the ship Bruce Ismay, the owner, decided to include only 16 wooden lifeboats and four collapsible boats. He concluded that this would be plenty of boats to "ferry passengers to a rescue ship. The [*Titanic*] should surely be able stay afloat long enough for help to arrive.... Why clutter the boat deck promenade with three dozen more boats than the law required?" (Matsen 104). If the lifeboats had all been filled to capacity before launch, over 1,000 people would still have perished that April night in 1912.

Even before the dark waters closed over the *Titanic,* the survivors began to wonder how this could have possibly happened? This ship was supposed to have been unsinkable! At the very least, it was supposed to act as its own life-boat like others before it, possibly for days, until help arrived. Once the news broke to the rest of the world, "the sheer dimensions of the *Titanic* disaster created sufficient public reaction on both sides of the Atlantic to prod reluctant governments into action, producing the first Safety of Life at Sea (SOLAS) convention in 1914" (International Ice Patrol, http://www.uscg-iip.org/cms/, 5-April-2010). The purpose of the resulting SOLAS Treaty, which has been continuously updated since 1914, is to "ensure that in the event of a catastrophe at sea passengers and crew have the greatest chance of survival" (International Ice Patrol, http://www.uscg-iip.org/cms/, 5-April-2010).

The SOLAS Convention's first order of business was to make official the International Ice Patrol (IIP) and to agree to new rules about how ships should deal with ice and especially icebergs. Within a few weeks after *Titanic* sank, the precursor to the IIP began the air reconnaissance of the ice lanes in the North Atlantic that continues today under the direction of the IIP. Its role is to investigate and communicate the ice conditions in the shipping lanes of the North Atlantic. In addition, when ice is reported by the IIP, ships are required to "proceed at moderate speed or alter course" (International Ice Patrol, http://www.uscg-iip.org/cms/, 5-April-2010).

In another change immediately after the loss of the *Titanic,* Harland & Wolff redesigned the expansion joints and steel reinforcement of its large ships. *Britannic* was *Titanic's* sister ship and was being built in dry dock at the time *Titanic* sank. During the summer of 2006, divers were able to reach the 400 feet where *Britannic* rests on the bottom of the Aegean Sea, after running into a mine during World War I. They discovered evidence that Harland & Wolff had significantly changed the expansion joint design on *Britannic* before she was commissioned (Matsen 261).

That the Harland & Wolff didn't announce this safety change to the world is testament to its fear of being sued by the families of the victims of the *Titanic* disaster. Secretly, quietly, without fanfare, the company decided on its own to "build *Britannic* with a double hull, and redesign the expansion joints and other weak points in the ships. There was no law that required it to do that. *Titanic* had perfectly conformed to the regulations of the British Board of Trade." (Matsen 241)

Also at the first SOLAS conference, new maritime communications regulations went into effect. Now it is required that ships have a telegraph (or communications) operator on duty around the clock who is part of the crew and reports directly to the captain. In another change, red rockets can only be used in cases of distress and "must be interpreted as a distress signal" by all ships in sight (International Ice Patrol, http://www.uscg-iip.org/cms/, 5-April-2010). After the *Titanic* sank, the telegraph (and now satellite communications) became primarily a safety feature on shipboard, rather than a communication service for passengers.

The most recognizable changes after the sinking were the significant new lifeboat requirements, which were specifically crafted to respond to those aspects of the *Titanic* disaster that caused unnecessary injury and death. Because the *Titanic* lifeboats were insufficient to evacuate all on board, the new SOLAS regulations required that all ships, both passenger and cargo, have enough lifeboats for all "souls" on board, plus rafts for an additional 25 percent. The extra life rafts can be used if all lifeboats have left the ship minimally loaded, as they did on the *Titanic*, and there are still people remaining aboard.

In addition to not having enough lifeboats, everyone was so complacent about *Titanic's* "unsinkability" that there had been no emergency lifeboat drills upon sailing. Worse than that, the officers and crew had not been properly trained to load and lower full lifeboats and they had no idea which lifeboats they had been assigned to. As a result, the new SOLAS Treaty required that "Abandon Ship" and "Fire Onboard" drills take place weekly on passenger ships and that there be regular and ongoing crew training (International Ice Patrol, http://www.uscg-iip.org/cms/, 5-April-2010). Anyone who has taken a cruise lately knows that these regulations are still in effect today.

The simplest change was the requirement that all ships have a public address system (International Ice Patrol, http://www.uscg-iip.org/cms/, 5-April-2010). Amazingly, *Titanic* did not have one, so most of the passengers were unclear what was happening as the ship went down.

Finally, in order to avoid the injuries that occurred as passengers from the *Titanic* attempted to jump into moving lifeboats, evacuation chutes, similar to those used on modern airplanes, were developed and are required to assist in the loading of the lifeboats. Many *Titanic* passengers who did make it to the lifeboats died of hypothermia and exposure, especially those who had become wet. As a result, the SOLAS Treaty requires that lifeboats on ships that sail the North Atlantic must be enclosed to provide protection from the cold and weather (International Ice Patrol, http://www.uscg-iip.org/cms/, 5-April-2010).

While everyone would have preferred the *Titanic* and all her passengers and crew to have enjoyed long lives, the shipping industry learned a great deal from the multiple errors and miscalculations that led to the appalling loss of life when the *Titanic* went down. In the wake of the disaster, new safety regulations went into effect and the International Ice Patrol was founded to provide information and track ice in the North Atlantic. Also, ships are now required to carry lifeboats for all on board and to drill passengers in how to use them.

Without the analysis resulting from the *Titanic* catastrophe, the shipping industry would not have had the information needed to make informed decisions about which improvements to implement to prevent a repeat disaster. The safety legacy of the *Titanic* still exists in the form of the lifeboat drills passengers participate in on the first day of each cruise. So when on a voyage and the lifeboat drill interrupts a dip in the pool, don't be annoyed. Instead, remember the alternative!

Words: 2259

ACTIVITY: Color-code each element of this essay. (i.e., lead-in, thesis, statement of structure, evidence, etc.) using a different color for each element. Then do the same for one of your own essays. Are all the elements represented? If any are missing, how could you add them?

THINKING & ORGANIZATION TOOLBOX

Happily, in all six types of expository writing, the writing process is the same, even though the content will vary dramatically. But sometimes it is hard to know where to begin researching and writing an essay. The following order of operations provides a path to follow in order to end up with a complete, balanced essay:

Topic provided or selected (p. 19)

⇓

Brainstorm information and ideas (pp. 24 & 31)

⇓

Determine text structure and transfer information from brainstorming session to appropriate analysis organizer (pp. 17 & 91, 97, 105, 114, 122, or 131)

⇓

Synthesize and summarize the patterns and relationships in the data on the analysis organizer to determine the thesis statement (p. 37)

⇓

Transfer this information to writing template (p. 86)

⇓

Use information on the analysis organizer to determine at least the three best supporting ideas and write summarizing supporitng idea statements (pp. 91, 97, 105, 114, 122, or 131)

⇓

Find evidence to explain the supporting ideas in detail (quotes, data, analysis of reliable experts, experimental results, mathematical processes, etc.) (pp. 43-54)

⇓

Reiterate and restate the thesis and supporting ideas in the conclusion (p. 60)

⇓

Write first draft: incorporate transitions to combine and explicitly explain the relationships and patterns between and among the ideas and evidence (p. 67)

⇓

Fully introduce, explain, and integrate terms and quotations (p. 43-54)

⇓

Write final draft: revising as needed, specifically tighten languge and streamline thinking (p. 74)

Ongoing Research (p. 25)

TEMPLATE: ORGANIZING EXPOSITORY WRITING

TOPIC: _____

BRAINSTORM/RESEARCH USING ANALYSIS ORGANIZER: _____

TEXT STRUCTURE: _____

Introduction
Lead-in (this is the universal concept that makes the specific thesis statement interesting to the audience):

Thesis Statement:

Statement of Structure: Implied? Explicit?

Supporting Idea I Summary Sentence:

Evidence:

Supporting Idea II Summary Sentence:

Evidence:

Supporting Idea III Summary Sentence:

Evidence:

Plus more supporting ideas as needed...

Conclusion

Restatement of thesis:

Recap of main points:

Universal application (see lead-in in introductory paragraph):

CHECKLIST: EDITING THE FINAL DRAFT

1. Remove slang, contractions, "text" spelling, and abbreviations.   DONE ☐

2. Remove first or second person (*I* or *you*) references.   DONE ☐

3. Ensure that quotes and evidence are introduced, explained, and integrated, not just dropped in randomly.   DONE ☐

4. Make sure quoted, paraphrased, and factual information is appropriately referenced using the relevant format (usually MLA format, but check with the person who assigned the task).   DONE ☐

5. Clearly show the relationship between and among ideas using appropriate and varied transition words and phrases.   DONE ☐

6. Use accurate punctuation to show the relationship between and among ideas.   DONE ☐

7. Replace imprecise words with precise vocabulary. Eliminate *thing, stuff, very, always, never, sort of, a lot*, etc.   DONE ☐

8. Confirm that verb tenses are consistent within the timeframe(s) being addressed.   DONE ☐

9. Check that all singular and plural subjects agree with their verbs.   DONE ☐

10. Spell all words correctly: look specifically at *their, there,* and *they're; to, too,* and *two;* and *it's* and *its*.   DONE ☐

11. Make sure the title communicates the thesis.   DONE ☐

Notes

TIPS FOR WRITING A COMPARE-CONTRAST ESSAY

A compare-contrast essay focuses on the similarities and differences between and among situations, processes, objects, or ideas. The purpose is to develop and explain the relationship between two or more items in order to better understand both.

Introduction

- ❖ Lead-in: How will this compare-contrast help someone better understand this topic? Why is this compare-contrast important in the big picture?

- ❖ Thesis statement: In a compare-contrast essay, the thesis statement needs to summarize the major similarities and differences in the topic and explain any relationships, if appropriate.

- ❖ Statement of structure: It can be implicit (incorporated into the thesis) or explicit (a stand-alone sentence)

Body of the Essay

The body paragraphs in a compare-contrast essay relate the similarities and differences between the two items being compared and are presented in one of two organizational formats:

- ❖ **Element-by-Element**
  One specific element of the first subject is presented and then the similar element of the second subject is presented. For example, if an essay is comparing two automobiles, safety features would probably be one of the elements of comparison. In an element-by-element approach, the safety features of each of the two vehicles would be discussed before addressing, for example, the cost of each car.

❖ **Subject-by-Subject**

In this method, all of the elements of the first automobile would be discussed before the elements of the second are presented. For example, a paragraph on the Geo Prism would include the car's safety features, cost, and performance record. The next paragraph on the Ford Escort would then include a comparison of the same elements in the same order.

IMPORTANT: When choosing similarities and differences, mention those that are the most important, the most descriptive, or the most informative. For example, when comparing-contrasting cars, focus on those elements that truly differentiate them based on their purpose. If a car's purpose is to move people and things from one place to another safely, car color is not that important. However, the difference in the power of the engines would be. Elaborate in such a way that similarities and differences are clear and distinct.

Transitions

Use transition words to help the reader follow the flow of ideas:

❖ <u>Transition words for similarities</u>
in a similar way, in the same manner, similarly, equally, equally as important, in the same fashion, likewise, in a like manner

❖ <u>Transition words for differences</u>
but, on the other hand, instead of, still, yet, although, in contrast to, whereas, nevertheless, rather, on the contrary

Conclusion

Exit the essay by restating the thesis, summarizing the main points, and then tying them in to the lead-in. Finally, end with a memorable idea—a relevant quotation, an interesting twist of logic, a call to action—related to the lead-in.

COMPARE-CONTRAST ANALYSIS ORGANIZER

TOPIC:

Critical Similarities	Critical Differences

Summary of Similarities:
- Classify/summarize the similarities.
- Is there a common thread among the similarities?
- How might the similarities be described?

Summary of Differences:
- Classify/summarize the differences.
- Is there a common thread among the differences?
- How might the differences be described?

Relationship: Is there a relationship between the similarities and differences? How do they influence each other?

Possible Thesis:

Compose Yourself!   www.lightbulblearning.net   page 91

COMPARE-CONTRAST ANALYSIS ORGANIZER

TOPIC: Compare and contrast the approaches of Malcolm X and Martin Luther King, Jr. to the African-American struggle for civil rights in the 1950s and 60s.

Critical Similarities

Both religious leaders (MLK Christian, MX Muslim)

Spoke out against racism

Personally faced violence

Their fight against racism polarized the nation

Both assassinated

Summary of Similarities:
- Classify/summarize the similarities.
- Is there a common thread among the similarities?
- How might the similarities be described?

Both committed to ending racism, no matter the personal danger

Relationship: Is there a relationship between the similarities and differences? How do they influence each other?

Different routes to the same goal. Ironic that the man who advocated non-violence (MLK) was also assassinated.

Critical Differences

MLK—advocated a non-violent approach to ending racism, favored a more incremental approach

MX—His motto for gaining equal rights was "By any means necessary!" and that included violence

Different religious beliefs

Summary of Differences:
- Classify/summarize the differences.
- Is there a common thread among the differences?
- How might the differences be described?

Methods of achieving an end to racism very different

Possible Thesis: While both Malcolm X and Martin Luther King, Jr. believed that racism and discrimination in the U.S. needed to be eradicated, they held opposing points of view on the role of violence in the struggle to convince white Americans to overcome their long-held beliefs.

SAMPLE COMPARE-CONTRAST TEMPLATE

TOPIC: Compare and contrast the approaches of Malcolm X and Martin Luther King, Jr. to the African-American struggle for civil rights in the 1950s and 60s.

BRAINSTORM (ON SEPARATE SHEET)

TEXT STRUCTURE: Compare-Contrast

Introduction

Lead-in (this is the universal concept that makes the specific thesis statement interesting): The Civil Rights movement of the 50s and 60s was one of the most necessary but divisive popular movements in American history. Given its continuing influence on current law and behavior, it is critical to understand how such momentous social change was achieved. Two of the most prominent African-American leaders within the movement were Malcolm X and Martin Luther King, Jr.

Thesis Statement: While both Malcolm X and Martin Luther King, Jr. believed that racism and discrimination in the U.S. needed to be eradicated, they held opposing points of view on the role of violence in the struggle to convince white Americans to overcome their long-held beliefs.

Statement of Structure: Implied

Supporting Idea I Summary Sentence: Both Malcolm X and Martin Luther King Jr. were angry about the continued racism and discrimination African-Americans throughout the nation were subjected to.

Evidence: Examine roots of racism in the U.S. and why it exists. Examples of institutionalized racism in the U.S. Quotes from each, introduced and explained.

Supporting Idea II Summary Sentence: Malcolm X believed the civil rights movement needed to be a violent armed struggle, as white Americans would not voluntarily give up their power over African-Americans.

Evidence: Quotes from Malcolm X and from others, introduced and explained

Supporting Idea III Summary Sentence: On the other hand, Martin Luther King, Jr. believed the civil rights movement must model non-violence and reflect Christian principles by treating all people, black or white, as children of God.

Evidence: Quotes from Martin Luther King, quotes from followers of Martin Luther King, Jr., introduced and explained

Conclusion
Restatement of thesis:

Recap of main points:

Universal application (see lead-in of introductory paragraph): These two men embodied the civil rights movement and encapsulated the fault lines within the movement itself. Their different philosophies are visible even today in political skirmishes involving affirmative action and voting rights.

TIPS FOR WRITING A CAUSE-EFFECT ESSAY

A cause-effect essay first presents a reason or motive for a particular event, situation or trend and then explains the results or consequences of that situation. The study of science and history most often use the cause-effect structure.

Introduction

- Lead-in: How will this cause-effect help someone better understand this topic? Why is this cause-effect topic important in the big picture?

- Thesis statement: In a cause-effect essay, the thesis statement needs to summarize the patterns and relationships within and between the most significant causes and effects related to the topic.

- Statement of structure: It can be implicit (incorporated into the thesis) or explicit (a stand-alone sentence)

Body of the Essay

Consider the following issues when constructing a cause-effect essay:

- ❖ To adequately present an event, condition, phenomenon, or trend, the writer must provide a reasonable background in order for the reader to understand the analysis. The degree of explanation depends on the complexity of the issue. If it is a simple situation, the writer might be able to explain it in the introduction. However, if it is a complex phenomenon, the writer might need to add a paragraph after the introduction that goes into more detail.

- ❖ A logical argument with evidence is necessary to persuade readers that the proposed causes or effects are reasonable, especially if they contradict previously accepted facts. To present such an argument, the writer must use sources that state facts and evidence. Examples and anecdotes can also be used, if appropriate.

IMPORTANT: When selecting causes and effects, choose those that are the most important, the most descriptive, or the most informative. For example, all ships on the North Atlantic the evening of April 14, 1912 had to contend with the same weather/light conditions. Not all ships ran into an iceberg and sank. So, while the weather conditions contributed to the sinking of the *Titanic*, they were not a primary cause.

Transitions

Use transition words to help the reader follow the flow of ideas:

> as a result, since, this led to, if....then, because, therefore, consequently, so that, in order to, occurrences, why, what, elements, factors

Conclusion

Exit the essay by restating the thesis, summarizing the main points, and then tying them into the lead-in. Finally, end with a memorable idea—a relevant quotation, an interesting twist of logic, a call to action—related to the lead-in.

CAUSE-EFFECT ANALYSIS ORGANIZER   TOPIC:

Causes/Reasons	Event/Situation	Effects/Results

Summary of Causes:
- Classify/summarize the causes.
- Is there a common thread or similarity among the causes?
- How might the causes be described?

Summary of Effects:
- Classify/summarize the effects.
- Is there a common thread or similarity among the effects?
- How might the effects be described?

Relationship: Is there a relationship between the causes and effects? How do they influence each other?

Possible Thesis:

Compose Yourself!   www.lightbulblearning.net   page 97

CAUSE-EFFECT ANALYSIS ORGANIZER

TOPIC: How did the decisions made at the end of World War I affect the likelihood of a lasting peace in Europe?

Causes/Reasons

Provisions of the Treaty of Versailles (ToV)

France's chief interests were national security, reparations, and the return of Alsace-Lorraine

Britain & the US wanted a restored Germany as an important trading partner and worried about the effect of reparations on the British economy

But the French won the fight to impose a harsh peace on Germany since it bore the brunt of the economic and physical destruction in the war

Event/Situation

End of WWI & terms of ToV

Germany to accept sole responsibility for causing the war and must:

Disarm completely

Make substantial territorial concessions

Pay brutal reparations to the Allies

Effects/Results

Of the ToV

Germany neither pacified, conciliated, nor permanently weakened

The ToV united Germans against the rest of Europe because they felt badly treated and unfairly accused of starting WWI (it was actually much more complicated than that)

Anti-Semitism grew because Germans erroneously thought (and were encouraged to believe) that German Jews had betrayed them

Huge burden of the reparations caused hyperinflation in Germany and common people suffered greatly

Resentment of the ToV resulted in fertile ground for the rise of the Nazi party

When Hitler became aggressive and broke the ToV he had the support of the German people

Compose Yourself!

www.lightbulblearning.net

CAUSE-EFFECT ANALYSIS ORGANIZER (CONT.)

Summary of Causes:
- Classify/summarize the causes.
- Is there a common thread or similarity among the causes?
- How might the causes be described?

Because WWI was so devastating for all involved, but especially the French, the Allies wanted German military and economic power to be significantly reduced. The ToV was revenge for Germany starting the war.

Summary of Effects:
- Classify/summarize the effects.
- Is there a common thread or similarity among the effects?
- How might the effects be described?

The ToV actually generated the conditions that led to another war—WWII. Rather than help the German people see the error of their ways, it just made them resentful. So they supported Hitler when he ignored the treaty and provoked Europe into another war.

Relationship: Is there a relationship between the causes and effects? How do they influence each other?

The intended effect of the ToV was the opposite of what actually occurred. The Allies wanted to create a permanent peace by destroying Germany's ability to make war, but instead Europe was at war again—WWII—within 20 years. So a man who survived fighting in WWI and made it home to his wife could have had an 18-19 year old son drafted to fight in WWII. How horrific!

Possible Thesis: Although the desire for revenge was understandable, the terms of the ToV, as dictated by the Allies, brutally punished Germany after World War I. These terms led directly to the rise of German political and military power in the 1930s and the subsequent breakout of World War II in 1939, just 20 years after the First World War ended.

SAMPLE CAUSE-EFFECT TEMPLATE

TOPIC: How did the decisions at the end of World War I affect the likelihood of a lasting peace Europe?

BRAINSTORM (ON SEPARATE SHEET)

TEXT STRUCTURE: Cause-Effect

Introduction

Lead-in (this is the universal concept that makes the specific thesis statement interesting): When one is wronged, it is human nature to want to exact revenge. This is true for nations as well as individuals. After the destruction visited on Europe during World War I, the Allies wanted to ensure that such a catastrophic war could never happen again. As they began to develop the terms of peace, the Allied powers kept this goal in mind. Unfortunately, it backfired.

Thesis Statement: Although the desire for revenge was understandable, the terms of the ToV, as dictated by the Allies, brutally punished Germany after World War I. Unfortunately, these terms led directly to the rise of the Nazi Party in the 1930s and ultimately the breakout of World War II in 1939.

Statement of Structure: Implied

Causes (or reasons) for the terms of the Treaty of Versailles

Supporting Idea I Summary Sentence: Because Germany was considered the aggressor in World War I, France feared a resurgence of a combative and war-bent German military power. Therefore, one of the terms of the ToV required Germany to disband its military and destroy all its heavy weapons.

Evidence: Data from the treaty, historical interpretations and analysis, participant accounts, contemporary newspaper articles, etc.

Supporting Idea II Summary Sentence: In addition, the ToV required Germany to pay enormous reparations to the Allies, effectively destroying the German economy. The war had destroyed the economy of Europe; France wanted to retaliate so that Germany would be unable to develop new weapons and rearm.

Evidence: Data from the treaty, historical interpretations and analysis, accounts of those affected, contemporary newspaper articles, etc.

Supporting Idea III Summary Sentence: Finally, France, Denmark, and Poland, among other countries, wanted land restored to them that Germany had seized in previous wars. The ToV returned contested land to all the Allied powers so affected.

Evidence: Data from the treaty, historical interpretations and analysis, eyewitness accounts, contemporary newspaper articles, etc.

Effects (or results) of WWI outcome on politics in Europe

Supporting Idea I Summary Sentence: As a result of the Treaty, Germany simply hid its military high command within another bureau of the government. Military leaders spent the years after WWI rewriting tactic and strategy manuals, taking into account lessons learned in WWI.

Evidence: Historical interpretations and analysis, participant accounts, contemporary documents, etc.

Supporting Idea II Summary Sentence: The economic fallout of the reparations caused hyperinflation, which greatly affected ordinary German citizens and increased general resentment against the former Allies.

Evidence: Historical interpretations and analysis, eyewitness accounts, contemporary newspaper articles, etc.

Supporting Idea III Summary Sentence: Regaining the land lost to the Allies in the ToV remained a rallying cry for the German people, who felt culturally German areas had been unfairly taken from them.

Evidence: Historical interpretations and analysis, participant accounts, contemporary newspaper articles, etc.

Conclusion
Restatement of thesis:

Recap of main points:

Universal application (see lead-in introductory paragraph): Often, taking desired revenge backfires on the avenger, both in one's personal life and in the political arena. The resentment and anger build up until there is an explosion. In the case of Europe in the 20th century, it erupted into another worldwide war, World War II, in 1939. Fortunately, the Allies did learn their lesson; after WWII ended, the Allied reaction was quite different towards the vanquished from the terms imposed by the Treaty of Versailles.

TIPS FOR WRITING A PROBLEM-SOLUTION ESSAY

A problem-solution essay addresses a complex philosophical dilemma with no clear right answer, develops criteria for addressing the problem, and informs readers about possible actions that might be taken to remedy the situation. No matter what sort of complex problem is encountered, the chances of solving it improve if it is approached analytically, conscious of the steps one can take and escape routes available if the steps become too rigid.

Introduction

- Lead-in: How will this problem-solution essay help someone better understand the problem and why it needs to be solved? Why is the solution(s) important in the big picture?

- Thesis statement: In a problem-solution essay, the thesis statement needs to summarize both the problem and the possible solution(s).

- Statement of structure: It can be implicit (incorporated into the thesis) or explicit (a stand-alone sentence)

The lead-in should answer the question, "What will happen if this problem is not solved?" The introduction needs to provide enough background information to understand the problem. Often that means at least one paragraph of the essay outlines the details of the problem as defined. Why is it a problem? What are the root causes? Does class reading and/or outside research provide any explanations?

BODY OF THE ESSAY

There are many facets to a problem-solution essay and all should be addressed:

- ❖ What is the alternative to solving the problem?

- ❖ What are the advantages and disadvantages of the alternative to solving the problem?

- ❖ What is the solution?

- ❖ How well is/will the solution work?

IMPORTANT: After describing the problem, the essay should outline a *realistic* solution. Begin by choosing one possibility. Assess any difficulties involved. Perhaps there are rules and regulations that need to be followed. Perhaps the solution will be prohibitively expensive. Where will the money come from? Discuss the solution in detail. Move onto other possibilities only after the first solution has been explained in full.

Transitions

Use transition words to help the reader follow the flow of ideas:
> the cause is, results are, corrected, improved, remedied, issue, possibilities, analysis, preferences, explanation, situation, obstacle, choice, outcome

Conclusion

Exit the essay by restating the thesis, summarizing the main points, and then tying them in to the lead-in. Finally, end with a memorable idea—a relevant quotation, an interesting twist of logic, a call to action—related to the lead-in.

PROBLEM-SOLUTION ANALYSIS ORGANIZER

TOPIC:

Describe Problem & Its Relative Importance	Develop Criteria for Solution(s)	Describe Solution(s) in Detail and Explain How It (They) Fulfills the Criteria	Consider Potential Problems/Arguments Raised by the Opposition and Refute

Relationship: Given the realities of today's world, is the solution(s) feasible? What is the best way to motivate others to adopt the solution(s)?

Possible Thesis: _____

_____

Compose Yourself!   www.lightbulblearning.net   page 105

PROBLEM-SOLUTION ANALYSIS ORGANIZER

TOPIC: How should healthcare in the United States be reformed?

Describe Problem & Its Relative Importance

Exponentially rising health care costs

Malignant influence of health insurance companies that deny coverage for a variety of spurious reasons

Many people in the U.S. are uninsured and sick or dying. Often they go bankrupt trying to get medical care

Develop Criteria for Solution(s)

Universal coverage, including no denial of coverage or service based on prior health conditions or current needs

Generally lower health care costs

Health decisions made by doctors, not insurance companies or government

Describe Solution(s) in Detail and Explain How It (They) Fulfills the Criteria

Regulate health coverage, whether private or public, similar to public utilities (electricity and water)

Mandatory universal access, including no denial of service allowed

Regulated rates kept affordable

Subsidies provided for those who can't pay

Consider Potential Problems/Arguments Raised by the Opposition and Refute

Who will pay? Universal coverage = more money in the pot

What about the current healthcare system? Convert it. The structure is already in place, just need to change the regulations

PROBLEM-SOLUTION ANALYSIS ORGANIZER (CONT.)

Relationship: Given the realities of today's world, is the solution(s) feasible? What is the best way to motivate people to adopt the solution(s)?

Solution is feasible; it is the utility industry model. However, the politics of the healthcare issue need to be addressed in order to convince both sides to adopt this solution.

Possible Thesis: The healthcare crisis in America has generated many suggestions for reform and a great deal of disagreement; however, one possible solution stands out. Treat healthcare like the necessity it is, with all the rules and regulations required of utilities like electrical, cable, water, and gas companies.

SAMPLE PROBLEM-SOLUTION TEMPLATE

TOPIC: How should healthcare in the United States be reformed?

BRAINSTORM (ON SEPARATE SHEET)

TEXT STRUCTURE: Problem-Solution

Introduction

Lead-in (this is the universal concept that makes the specific thesis statement interesting): One issue on which Democrats and Republicans concur on is that finding a solution to the healthcare crisis is the most important item on the agenda of this Congress. However, that is about all the members of Congress agree on. The opposing political views on the role of government have obscured the need to act. However, there is already a model of government involvement that could serve as a template to solve the healthcare dilemma.

Thesis Statement: The healthcare crisis in America has generated many suggestions for reform and a great deal of disagreement; however, one possible solution stands out. Treat healthcare like the necessity it is, with all the rules and regulations required of utilities like electrical, cable, water, and gas companies.

Statement of Structure: Implied

Define/explain problem: Explain how the healthcare crisis evolved.

Evidence: Statistics showing rise in healthcare costs and premiums, numbers of uninsured, anecdotes of healthcare gone awry.

Supporting Idea I Summary Sentence: In order to prevent price gouging, the prices public utilities can charge customers are regulated, often within a marketplace.

Evidence: Relate details of price regulations in the utility sector and show how it could be applied to the healthcare industry.

Supporting Idea II Summary Sentence: In addition to regulating prices, public utilities are required to provide access to all; they cannot pick and choose which neighborhoods to service.

Evidence: Relate details of access in the utility sector and show how it could be applied to the healthcare industry.

Supporting Idea III Summary Sentence: Utility companies' services are also regulated so that a basic minimum of services is offered to all customers. Often additional customer benefits can be added, but at an additional cost to the customer. Apply the same principal to the healthcare industry.

Evidence: Relate details of services in the utility sector and show how it could work in to the healthcare industry.

Conclusion
Restatement of thesis:

Recap of main point:

Universal application (see lead-in introductory paragraph): Perhaps if Congress would put politics aside and analyze an existing example of government involvement in the market place, it could find a mutually agreeable solution to the most important issue to face Americans in a generation.

TIPS FOR WRITING A CONCEPT-DEFINITION ESSAY

A concept-definition essay provides a personal (but still factually complete and correct) understanding of a particular concept or term. The essay conveys what research, understanding, and experience have taught the writer about the concept or term. What a concept "is not" is often part of the definition.

INTRODUCTION

- Lead-in: How will this concept-definition essay help someone better understand the concept? Why is understanding the concept important in the big picture?

- Thesis statement: In a concept-definition essay the thesis statement must provide a summary definition of the concept.

- Statement of structure: It can be implicit (incorporated into the thesis) or explicit (a stand-alone sentence)

BODY OF THE ESSAY

The purpose of a concept-definition essay is to define a concept. A definition can be developed in a number of ways, some of which mimic other text structures. That is OK. If the definition requires an explanation of cause-effect, so be it. The introduction and conclusion will focus the reader on the concept-definition purpose of the essay.

As an example, consider a definition of a cultural concept such as professional sports:

- ❖ The essay could begin with a **history** (a kind of process essay) of the development of professional sports in American culture, its migration to other countries, its growth and transformation into entertainment, its excesses and successes.

- It could include **examples** of the types of professional sports and the success and failure of various leagues.

- It could describe professional sports as a **process** (the steps involved to create a league or team) or develop an **analysis** of its principles and its place in American culture.

- It could provide a **contrast** to other countries' professional sports leagues, demonstrating what American professional sports are and are not.

- It could even be structured as a **cause-effect** explanation, describing how professional sports respond to certain needs in modern American culture or how American culture is influenced by sports.

A concept-definition essay is not limited to any one method of development and it may employ more than one text structure simultaneously.

Another way to define something is to explain what it is not. When defining the idea of "home," one could begin by suggesting that the adage "There's no place like home" is silly because there are, in fact, many places like home. Or one could insist that home is not really a place at all, but an idea.

IMPORTANT: Some rhetorical points about definitions:
- Avoid using the phrases "is where" and "is when": A professional sport _is when_ gifted athletes are paid to play a sport as a job. Or A computer virus _is where_....
- Avoid circular definitions (repeating the defined term within the definition itself). A computer _virus is a virus_ that destroys or disrupts software.
- Avoid using a too narrow definition, one that would unduly limit the scope of the essay. Reggae music is sung on the Caribbean island of Jamaica. In fact, reggae music is sung all over the world, although it was born in Jamaica.

TRANSITIONS

Use transition words to help the reader follow the flow of ideas:

> examples are, described as, looks like, critical attributes are, functions like, who, what, where, when, description, characteristics, issues, process, explanation

CONCLUSION

Exit the essay by restating the thesis, summarizing the main points, and then tying them in to the lead-in. Finally, end with a memorable idea—a relevant quotation, an interesting twist of logic, a call to action—related to the lead-in.

CONCEPT-DEFINITION ANALYSIS ORGANIZER

TOPIC:

Dictionary or Subject-Area Definition:

Critical Elements of the Concept	Why Is this Concept Important?	How/When Is the Concept Used?	Counter Examples

Relationship: What are some examples of this concept in action? Are there any analogies that help illustrate this concept?

Possible Thesis:

CONCEPT-DEFINITION ANALYSIS ORGANIZER

TOPIC: Does Odysseus fulfill the role of an ancient Greek hero?

Dictionary or Subject-Area Definition:
The ancient Greek hero undergoes some sort of ordeal. The hero, who is mortal, not immortal like the gods, must suffer during his or her lifetime and must die. He must struggle against his fear of death in order to achieve the most perfect end to his life. Only after death can the hero receive immortalization through veneration in cult and in song.

Critical Elements of the Concept (a Greek Hero)

Is mortal, not immortal

Lives to the extreme, in both good and bad ways

Has a ritually antagonistic relationship with the god or goddess most like him/her. This relationship is a fatal attraction

Suffers and dies

Eternal honor in dying well, in contrast to doing good while alive

Why Is This Concept Important?

All cultures have heroes

Humans want to admire individuals who achieve great things

Different cultures define heroic actions differently. It's important to know which definition of hero is being used

How/When Is the Concept Used?

The stories about ancient heroes occur mostly when studying literature, archeology, and history

These stories also help people assess their own behavior and establish what is important to them in life

Counter Examples

Odysseus, since he doesn't die and by Greek standards is not particularly extreme in his behavior

Modern heroes, because they are required to exemplify good moral standards

CONCEPT-DEFINITION ANALYSIS ORGANIZER (CONT.)

Relationship: What are some examples of this concept in action? Are there any analogies that help illustrate this concept?

Achilles, Hercules, Oedipus

Possible Thesis: Because the ancient Greek hero is a morally ambiguous figure who undergoes an ordeal that requires a struggle against the fear of death but who ultimately dies, Odysseus does not qualify as a hero in the Greek sense.

TOPIC: Does Odysseus fulfill the role of an ancient Greek hero?

BRAINSTORM (ON SEPARATE SHEET)

TEXT STRUCTURE: Concept-Definition

Introduction

Lead-in (this is the universal concept that makes the specific thesis statement interesting): Every culture has its heroes and heroines and their struggles define the important attributes of that culture. In fact, scholars often learn about the beliefs and desires of a culture by studying it heroes and heroines.

Thesis: Because the traditional ancient Greek hero is a morally ambiguous figure who undergoes an ordeal in which he struggles against the fear of death but ultimately dies, Odysseus does not qualify as a hero in the Greek sense.

Statement of Structure: Implied

Supporting Idea I Summary Sentence: Ancient Greek heroes are extreme in both good ways and bad; moral focus is not what defines them.

Evidence: Lives of Achilles, Oedipus

Supporting Idea II Summary Sentence: Ancient Greek heroes are frequently in conflict with the gods. This antagonism often results in their deaths or eternal torture.

Evidence: Life of Prometheus

Supporting Idea III Summary Sentence: Greek heroes find eternal honor in dying well, not necessarily in living a morally good life.

Evidence: Life of Hercules

Conclusion

Restatement of thesis:

Recap of main point:

Universal application (see lead-in introductory paragraph): The focus of ancient Greek heroes and culture is on the eternal, rather than the immediate. Strength, bravery, and loyalty were the characteristics valued in ancient Greece. It never mattered whether these attributes were used to good or bad effect. This is very unlike our modern concept of a hero as someone who lives an exemplary life.

TIPS FOR WRITING A GOAL-ACTION-OUTCOME (PROCESS) ESSAY

A goal-action-outcome essay either tells the reader how to do something or describes how something is done. There are two types of process essays: those that instruct and those that explain or analyze. The goal-action-outcome pattern of organization is especially important in scientific and mathematical writing. For example, it is used to describe biological processes like T-cell lymphocyte production, chemical processes like drug interactions, and technical processes like a colonoscopy. In mathematics it is used to explain how to solve complex, real-world, multi-step math problems.

INTRODUCTION

- Lead-in: How will this goal-action-outcome essay help someone better understand how or why something is done? *Why is doing/knowing it important in the big picture?*

- Thesis statement: A goal-action-outcome thesis statement articulates a clear goal and the reason for the goal.

- Statement of structure: It can be implicit (incorporated into the thesis) or explicit (a stand-alone sentence)

State what the goal-action-outcome is and why it is important:

> The digestive process is critical in providing living organisms with the needed energy to maintain life.

Provide background information in the form of the statement of structure (see *Statement of Structure* section) and define the goal-action-outcome that will be explained:

> A group of <u>organs, the mouth, esophagus, stomach, and intestines,</u> work together to perform the complex task of digestion, which includes the process of breaking down food from large molecules into small ones to make it easier to absorb as energy.

BODY OF THE ESSAY

When writing a goal-action-outcome (process) essay, consider the following:

- ❖ What process is being explained? Why is it important?

- ❖ Who or what does the process affect?

- ❖ Are there different ways of completing the process? If so, what are they?

- ❖ Who are the readers? What additional knowledge do they need to understand this process, if any?

- ❖ What skills/equipment are needed for this process to be completed, if any?

- ❖ How long does the process take? Is the outcome always the same?

- ❖ How many steps complete the process?

- ❖ Why is each step important?

- ❖ What difficulties are encountered in each step, if any? How can they be overcome?

- ❖ Are any cautions necessary?

- ❖ Does the process have definitions that need to be clarified?

- ❖ Are there other processes that are similar and more familiar to the audience that could help illustrate this process?

- ❖ If needed, tell what should or should not be done when completing the process and why.

IMPORTANT: Clarity is critical. When writing a goal-action-outcome essay, the reader should be able to replicate the process (if it is physically possible!) or visualize it well enough to explain it to someone else.

TRANSITIONS

Use transition words to help the reader follow the flow of ideas:

accomplish, steps taken, effects are, achieving, purpose is, steps, results, product, begin, process, first (second, third, etc.), next, finally

CONCLUSION

Exit the essay by restating the thesis, summarizing the main points, and then tying them in to the lead-in. Finally, end with a memorable idea—a relevant quotation, an interesting twist of logic, a call to action—related to the lead-in.

GOAL-ACTION-OUTCOME ANALYSIS ORGANIZER

GOAL:

Reason for or Purpose of Goal	Step-by-Step Actions to Reach Goal	Potential Pitfalls	Desired Outcome
• Why is this goal important? • What are the consequences of success? • What are the consequences of failure?	The reader should be able to recreate the actions from the text alone, based on the action plan.	• What might go wrong at each step? • What will be hard to do and why? • Detail any helpful hints.	• Describe the perfect outcome. • Will following these steps obtain the perfect outcome? Why or why not? • What are the "lessons learned"?

Possible Goal Statement:

Compose Yourself!

GOAL-ACTION-OUTCOME ANALYSIS ORGANIZER

GOAL: To develop a personal fitness plan.

Reason for/ Purpose of Goal	Step-by-Step Actions to Reach Goal	Potential Pitfalls	Desired Outcome
• Why is this goal important? • What are the consequences of success? • What are the consequences of failure? Want to play varsity football Don't want to get injured Want to get and remain healthy, not get sick	The reader should be able to re-create the actions from the text alone, based on the action plan. Create day-by-day cardio plan to follow from now until the season starts Develop day-by-day weightlifting plan to increase strength from now until the season starts Establish a reasonable nutrition plan that I can realistically follow Perhaps use a calendar to plan out the 3 strands	• What might go wrong at each step? • What will be hard to do and why? • Detail any helpful hints. I might get lazy and not keep up with my daily workouts I might get injured while training—then I'd have to stop and I'd get behind schedule I might not stick with my nutrition plan and continue to eat junk food	• Describe the perfect outcome. • Will following these steps obtain the perfect outcome? Why or why not? • What are the "lessons learned"? To be ready for football season To surprise my coach To prove to myself that I have the discipline to follow a long-term plan

Possible Goal Statement: Because fitness and strength are critical when playing contact sports, especially varsity football, this fitness plan will focus on enhancing cardiovascular endurance and strength and improving nutrition.

SAMPLE GOAL-ACTION-OUTCOME TEMPLATE

TOPIC: Develop a personal fitness plan.

BRAINSTORM (ON SEPARATE SHEET)

TEXT STRUCTURE: Goal-Action-Outcome

Introduction

Lead-in (this is the universal concept that makes the specific thesis statement interesting): Personal goals are critical when a person wants to achieve mightily in life, and the ability to focus and plan for achievement begins in high school. The feeling of accomplishment after reaching a difficult goal is worth the required effort.

Thesis: Because fitness and strength are critical when playing contact sports, especially varsity football, this fitness plan will focus on cardiovascular endurance and strength and enhancing nutrition.

Statement of Structure: Implied

Supporting Idea I Summary Sentence: The first element of this fitness plan is to improve and increase cardiovascular capacity.

Evidence: Day-by-day plan for building up cardio capacity gradually to avoid injury. Perhaps include a calendar at the end with the three elements mapped out daily.

Supporting Idea II Summary Sentence: Once cardiovascular capacity is improving, begin to build overall body strength.

    Evidence: Day-by-day weight lifting plan to gradually build up strength to avoid injury. Perhaps include a calendar at the end with all three elements mapped out daily.

Supporting Idea III Summary Sentence: As a result of increased overall fitness, one's body begins to crave nutritious food. However, there may still be a desire to cheat sometimes, so developing an appealing and effective nutrition plan is essential.

    Evidence: Description of an athlete's nutritionally balanced diet, including day-by-day healthy menus and a food journal.

Conclusion

Restatement of thesis:

Recap of main point:

Universal application (see lead-in introductory paragraph): This plan must to be followed closely in order to produce the goal of being a first-string member of the varsity football team in the fall. It is the initial step to improving athletic performance and becoming the best athlete possible.

Notes

Tips for Writing a Proposition-Support (Persuasive) Essay

"Proposition" is a fancy word for argument. The purpose of a proposition-support essay is to be as convincing as possible, and to convince readers to accept the proposition as true. A proposition-support essay uses logic, reason, and evidence to show that one idea is more legitimate than another. The argument must always use sound reasoning and solid evidence by stating facts, giving logical reasons, using examples, and quoting reliable experts. Though the goal is to convince others that a thesis statement is valid, it is important to remember that reasonable people can disagree. The act of writing the essay should help both the writer and the reader to examine their own and others' assumptions and ideas more carefully. Writing a proposition-support essay helps students to weigh evidence, clearly state ideas, fairly consider the claims of the opposition, and justify the position taken.

It is critically important that the tone of a proposition-support essay be reasonable, and that the presentation be factual and believable. Additionally, although this type of essay reflects the writer's opinion, the first-person point of view is not appropriate in analytical essays.

Consider the following sentences:

> ~~I believe that~~ all school students should wear uniforms.
>
> All school students should wear uniforms.

The first sentence uses the first person. This would work in a narrative, but here it limits the meaning of the sentence to just the writer, and it makes the writer sound weak—as if she is justifying herself. The second sentence is much more forceful. It makes a statement and does not restrict itself to only what the writer believes.

IMPORTANT: A convincing argument does the following:

- ❖ Anticipates and refutes reader objections in advance; and

- ❖ Uses an objective, reasonable tone.

It is never wise to attack a reader:

It is obvious that Americans must be able to legally carry concealed weapons. The power of the crazy anti-gun lobby to block gun ownership has created an unsafe environment.

In this example, by stating, "It is obvious" the writer insults the reader's intelligence in advance. Then the writer reverts to name-calling ("crazy"), a further insult to those who support gun control. It could all be true, but why should the reader accept the premise?

Compare:

Given the increase in gun violence on the streets of the United States, Congress would be wise to consider a federal law allowing all U.S. citizens to carry concealed weapons in public. The Constitution provides for this right and if private citizens carry guns, then criminals would think twice before victimizing the community.

It's important to be fair and to keep the writing voice modulated, reasonable, and as objective as possible. Do not insult the reader!

IMPORTANT: A writer, thinker, learner should be able to effectively argue both sides on an argument—no matter his personal opinion or beliefs. In fact, it is good practice to write the opposing argument; it strengthens the writer's understanding of the issue and helps her to intelligently, rather than emotionally, rebut opposition arguments.

INTRODUCTION

- Lead-in: How will this proposition-support essay help someone better understand the proposition and agree with it? Why is agreement important in the big picture?

- Thesis statement: In a proposition-support essay, the thesis statement needs to express a clear point-of-view or opinion—no wishy-washy thesis statements allowed!

- Statement of structure: It can be implicit (incorporated into the thesis) or explicit (a stand-alone sentence).

BODY OF THE ESSAY

Identify the areas that need to be addressed. Use statistics, research, real-life experiences, and/or examples from credible experts to support the argument. Some options for organization include the following:

- ❖ Generate a hypothetical instance: Used particularly when the writer wants the reader to consider a different point of view.

- ❖ Clarify a position: Differentiate between what information needs to be explained and what can be assumed.

- ❖ Think through a process to propose an improvement: Dissect the procedure from start to finish, providing any background information a reader might need.

- ❖ Analyze: Look at the parts of the proposition to help the reader to better understand the whole issue.

- ❖ Draw an analogy: Explain or elaborate on an idea by identifying significant likenesses between two objects, situations, or ideas when otherwise they are quite different. This is particularly helpful when the comparison is made to something familiar to the reader.

IMPORTANT: The goal is to convince the opposition! In order to write an effective proposition-support essay, the writer must anticipate and overcome objections that an adversary might raise. Ask these questions:

- ❖ What are the strongest, most compelling arguments made against this proposition?

- ❖ How can the writer defend this proposition against these arguments?

- ❖ What are the argument's weakest points?

- ❖ What are the weak links in the opposition's thinking?

Don't try to look good by mentioning only weaker opposition arguments. When defending the con side of the argument, try to view the issue through the eyes of the adversaries and draw out the best ideas they might use against the original proposition. Think about how to refute the opposition's justifications. Once those arguments have been addressed, check the original proposition to see if it needs revision.

TRANSITIONS
Use transition words to help the reader follow the flow of ideas:
> sufficient evidence, conclusion, viewpoint, opinion, topic is, belief, idea, hypotheses, theory, proof, logic, research, expert verification, reason

CONCLUSION
Exit the essay by restating the thesis, summarizing the main points, and then tying them in to the lead-in. Finally, end with a memorable idea—a relevant quotation, an interesting twist of logic, a call to action—related to the lead-in.

PROPOSITION-SUPPORT ANALYSIS ORGANIZER

TOPIC:

Pros	Cons

Summary of Pros:
- Classify/summarize the pros.
- Is there a common thread among the pros?
- How might the pros be described?

Summary of Cons:
- Classify/summarize the cons.
- Is there a common thread among the cons?
- How might the cons be described?

Relationship: Does a relationship exist between the pros and cons? How do they influence each other? Can the cons be mitigated? Can there be pros without cons?

Possible Thesis:

What Arguments Might Be Raised Against the Thesis? (Look at Pros and Cons)

PROPOSITION-SUPPORT ANALYSIS ORGANIZER

TOPIC: Is playing video games detrimental to academic achievement?

Pros of playing video games

Active imaginative engagement, not like watching TV

Requires decision-making, problem-solving skills

Consequences to actions in game

Develops persistence

Cons of playing video games

Too much time inside watching TV

Games are violent

Don't accomplish anything real

It's a waste of time

Used to avoid doing "real" things

Summary of Pros:
- Classify/summarize the pros.
- Is there a common thread among the pros?
- How might the pros be described?

The pros of playing video games are actually what teachers and parents say they want kids to do—solve problems, develop persistence, and understand consequences.

Summary of Cons:
- Classify/summarize the cons.
- Is there a common thread among the cons?
- How might the cons be described?

The cons of playing video games are similar to those of reading–passive, can show violence, can be used as an excuse to waste time and procrastinate. Also, academic work doesn't accomplish anything "real" either.

PROPOSITION-SUPPORT ANALYSIS ORGANIZER (CONT.)

Relationship: Does a relationship exist between the pros and cons? How do they influence each other? Can there be pros without cons?

The cons seem to involve a misunderstanding about what video games require of players. Have the people who denigrate video games ever actually played them?

Possible Thesis: Contrary to popular belief, playing video games actually enhances positive academic behaviors, honing decision-making and problem-solving skills, persistence, and the understanding of consequences.

What Arguments Might Be Raised Against the Thesis? (Look at Pros and Cons)

The cons seem to involve a misunderstanding about what video games require of players. Will need to include lots of examples from actual video games to refute this argument. Also, there will always be unbalanced people who will misunderstand or abuse the representations of violence on video games, television shows, etc. They need help, its true, but banning video games is not the way to solve the problem.

TOPIC: Is playing video games detrimental to academic achievement?

BRAINSTORM (ON SEPARATE SHEET)

TEXT STRUCTURE: Proposition-Support

Introduction

Lead-in (this is the universal concept that makes the specific thesis statement interesting): How many times have parents and teachers discussed the detrimental effects video games have on students' educational and interpersonal development? Too many to count. What they do not realize is that they could not be more wrong about their assumptions.

Thesis: Contrary to popular belief, playing video games actually enhances positive academic behaviors, honing decision-making and problem-solving skills, persistence, and the understanding of consequences.

Statement of Structure: Implied

Supporting Idea I Summary Sentence: The choices a player has to make to move up to the next level require split-second decision-making. Similarly, in order to work though the mistakes that have prevented a high score, the player must engage in complex problem solving.

Evidence: Examples from specific games. Video games not passive like reading and watching TV.

Supporting Idea II Summary Sentence: Many teachers and parents complain of a lack of persistence in the younger generation. They obviously have not watched students play video games. Players spend hours experimenting, practicing, and improving their skills so they can succeed.

Evidence: Specific examples of hours spent playing and what it accomplished. Can transfer this persistence to schoolwork.

Supporting Idea III Summary Sentence: Even though some video games can be violent, there are always consequences to actions taken when playing.

Evidence: Examples from specific games. There will always be those few people who cannot differentiate between pretend and real violence and these types of people will never change heir attitude. It's nothing new.

Conclusion
Restatement of thesis:

Recap of main point:

Universal application (see lead-in introductory paragraph): Playing video games is actually beneficial to one's academic achievement. So play on!

Notes

RUBRICS FOR ASSESSMENT

All written work should be assessed using a rubric—that is, a set of criteria linked to standards and used to assess a student's performance on papers, projects, essays, and other complex assignments. Detailed rubrics allow for more uniform instruction and evaluation according to specified criteria, making assessment simpler and more transparent.

The rubric informs the student what is important about the assignment. It allows teachers and students alike to learn and assess the criteria, self-reflect, and participate in peer review. Although not perfect, rubrics encourage accurate and fair assessment, deep student understanding, and thoughtful reflection on subsequent learning and teaching. The following diagnostic rubrics have been created for secondary teachers involved in the *FLEX Team* process to use with each text structure. However, they are effective even when not linked to *FLEX Team* analysis.

For additional information about *FLEX Teams*, see www.aypconsulting.org.

The rubrics listed are for ninth grade cross-curricular writing. If ninth grade writers are proficient according to these rubrics, then students, teachers and parents alike will be happy! Each grade level can develop its own rubrics using those provided as a guide.

Start with a four-point rubric: *Exemplary* (4), *Proficient* (3), *Zone of Proximal Development* (2), and *Significant Reteaching* (1). In all rubric writing, begin by describing the criteria for proficient—*not* average—work. It is impossible to know what is *Exemplary* or *Zone of Proximal Development* writing when unclear about what students need to know and be able to do in order to be considered proficient.

After determining the qualitative characteristics of a proficient paper (not quantitative, not "limited to seven grammar mistakes" [quantitative], but rather "expresses a clear thesis statement" [qualitative]), develop the description of an essay that is still in the *Zone of Proximal Development (ZPD)*. The ZPD describes the difference between what a learner can do without help and what he can accomplish with assistance. Sometimes it is referred to as "using but confusing" concepts and skills or "close, but not quite." No one becomes proficient at anything without moving through her ZPD first.

The concept of scaffolding is closely related to ZPD. Scaffolding is a process through which a teacher or more competent peer gives aid to students in their ZPD as necessary and tapers this aid as it becomes unnecessary, just as a scaffold is removed from a building during construction.

Proficient and *ZPD* are the two most important levels of written work to describe because they determine which students can continue to practice writing independently and which require some reteaching. Those students writing and thinking at the ZPD level will need some reteaching of the knowledge or skills they are "using but confusing." Once these two indicators are in place, describing an essay in the *Significant Reteaching* range is relatively simple; it has few or none of the qualities described as proficient.

Only after determining the *Proficient*, *ZPD*, and *Significant Reteaching* descriptions of student work can an *Exemplary* piece of work be described. This is because *Exemplary* does *not* indicate the writing is "above and beyond." It is not fair to students to declare that the only way to score at the *Exemplary* level is to do things the teacher did not teach them how to do. What differentiates an *Exemplary* essay from one that is simply *Proficient* is concise thinking and writing. These are the essays that say only what is necessary and no more, no less. Students who are writing at this level are using cumulative subject-area vocabulary, precise general vocabulary, and sophisticated and transparent transition language. The only way to move to the *Exemplary* level is to become proficient and then practice, practice, practice. This is why it is so critical for *all* teachers to assign some writing in their classrooms and why the focus in this guide is on proficient, rather than exemplary, writing.

Within the four performance levels, the criteria are divided into four distinct areas:

- ❖ **Structure of Argument**—Does the essay have a clear thesis statement and appropriate supporting evidence? Does it lead the reader through the argument effectively? This is the only part of the rubric that changes slightly from text structure to text structure.

- ❖ **Use of Language**—Is the language appropriate for the purpose, audience, and subject area? Is it formal, clear, and correct?

- ❖ **Knowledge of Concept/Facts**—Does the essay accurately describe, explain, and incorporate appropriate subject-area facts and concepts?

- ❖ **Integration/Quality of Analysis**—Does the essay make connections between and among ideas and concepts and appropriately apply ideas to real-world examples discussed in class?

General Rubric

This is a general analytical writing rubric. Specific "Structure of Argument" rubrics for each of the six different text structures follow.

Exemplary	Proficient

Exemplary

❖ **Structure of Argument**—Thesis statement is appropriate and concise; supporting evidence is well-chosen and transparently leads the reader through the argument:
- Tight, analytical thesis statement;
- At least three relevant and noteworthy supporting ideas;
- Pertinent evidence supports argument; and
- Relevant and sophisticated transition language effortlessly leads the reader through the argument.

❖ **Use of Language**—The language is sophisticated, precise, and appropriate for the purpose, audience, and subject area:
- Cumulative subject-area vocabulary and precise general vocabulary; and
- Formal academic language with recognizable and appropriate style and voice.

❖ **Knowledge of Concept/Facts**—Author accurately describes, explains, and incorporates sophisticated subject-area facts and concepts.

❖ **Integration/Quality of Ideas**—Makes unusual connections between and among ideas and concepts, applies and extends ideas discussed in class to real-world examples.

Proficient

❖ **Structure of Argument**—Thesis statement is clear and there is appropriate supporting evidence to lead the reader through the argument effectively:
- Well-defined, analytical thesis statement;
- At least three relevant supporting ideas;
- Pertinent evidence supports argument; and
- Appropriate transition language leads the reader through the argument.

❖ **Use of Language**—The language is appropriate for the purpose, audience, and subject area:
- Relevant general and subject-area vocabulary;
- Formal academic language;
- Analytical, unemotional, language; and
- Suitable transition language that leads reader through argument.

❖ **Knowledge of Concept/Facts**—Author accurately describes, explains, and applies useful subject-area facts and concepts.

❖ **Integration/Quality of Ideas**—Writer makes appropriate connections between and among ideas and concepts, transfers ideas discussed in class to real-world examples.

General Rubric (cont.)

Zone of Proximal Development	Significant Reteaching

Zone of Proximal Development

❖ **Structure of Argument**—Thesis statement is partial, non-analytical, or wishy-washy; there is some supporting evidence, and some attempt to lead the reader through the argument.

❖ **Use of Language**—Language is often, but not always, appropriate for the purpose, audience, and subject area.

❖ **Knowledge of Concept/Facts**—Author partially describes, explains, and uses pertinent subject-area facts and concepts.

❖ **Integration/Quality of Ideas**—Writer makes some connections between and among ideas and concepts and attempts to apply ideas, which may or may not be relevant or appropriate, to real-world examples.

Significant Reteaching

❖ **Structure of Argument**—There is no clear thesis statement, no clear supporting evidence, and no organizational structure.

❖ **Use of Language**—Language is inappropriate for the purpose, audience, and subject area.

❖ **Knowledge of Concept/Facts**—Little or no description, explanation, or application of appropriate subject-area facts and concepts included.

❖ **Integration/Quality of Ideas**—No or irrelevant connections between and among ideas and concepts and no effort made to apply ideas discussed in class to real-world examples.

SPECIFIC STRUCTURE OF ARGUMENT CRITERIA FOR EACH TEXT STRUCTURE

Compare-Contrast Structure of Argument Criteria

Exemplary

The essay includes a concise thesis statement, appropriate and well-chosen supporting evidence, and transparently leads the reader through the argument:

- Concisely explains how the compare-contrast can help someone better understand the ideas/objects being compared and why this is important in the big picture, making insightful connections in the process;
- Begins with a concise, analytical thesis statement that effectively summarizes the most critical similarities and differences in the topic;
- Includes at least three appropriate and exceptional supporting ideas;
- Uses relevant and well-chosen evidence to support the argument; and
- Employs accurate transition language to effortlessly lead the reader through the argument.

Proficient

The essay includes a well-defined thesis statement, appropriate supporting evidence, and effectively leads the reader through the argument:

- Clearly explains how the compare-contrast will help someone better understand the ideas/objects being compared and why topic is important in the big picture;
- Begins with a clear, analytical thesis statement that effectively summarizes the major similarities and differences in the topic;
- Includes at least three appropriate supporting ideas;
- Uses pertinent evidence to support argument; and
- Employs relevant transition language to lead the reader through the argument effectively.

Zone of Proximal Development

The essay includes only a partial thesis statement and/or some supporting evidence.

Significant Reteaching

The essay includes little or no thesis statement, little or no supporting evidence, and does not lead the reader through the argument.

Cause-Effect Structure of Argument Criteria

Exemplary

The essay includes a concise thesis statement, appropriate and well-chosen supporting evidence, and transparently leads the reader through the argument:

- Concisely explains how the causes and/or effects help someone better understand this topic *AND* why this topic is important in the big picture, making insightful connections;
- Has a concise, analytical thesis statement that summarizes the patterns and relationships within and between the most significant causes and/or effects related to the topic;
- Has at least three appropriate and exceptional supporting ideas;
- Has appropriate and well-chosen evidence used to support argument; and
- Uses relevant transition language to transparently lead the reader through the argument.

Proficient

The essay includes a well-defined thesis statement, appropriate supporting evidence, and effectively leads the reader through the argument:

- Clearly explains how the causes and/or effects help someone better understand this topic and why this topic is important in the big picture;
- Begins with a clear, analytical thesis statement that summarizes the patterns and relationships within and between the most significant causes and/or effects related to the topic;
- Includes at least three appropriate supporting ideas;
- Uses pertinent evidence to support argument; and
- Employs relevant transition language to lead the reader through the argument effectively.

Zone of Proximal Development

The essay includes only a partial thesis statement and/or some supporting evidence.

Significant Reteaching

The essay includes little or no thesis statement, little or no supporting evidence, and does not lead the reader through the argument.

Problem-Solution Structure of Argument Criteria

Exemplary

The essay includes a concise thesis statement, appropriate and well-chosen supporting evidence, and transparently leads the reader through the argument:

- Concisely explains how the problem-solution essay can help someone better understand the problem, why it needs to be solved, why the solution(s) is important in the big picture, making insightful connections in the process;
- Begins with a concise, analytical thesis statement summarizing both the problem and the possible solution(s).
- Includes at least three appropriate and exceptional supporting ideas;
- Uses pertinent and well-chosen evidence to support argument; and
- Employs accurate transition language to effortlessly lead the reader through the argument.

Proficient

The essay includes a well-defined thesis statement, appropriate supporting evidence, and effectively leads the reader through the argument:

- Clearly explains how the problem-solution essay can help someone better understand the problem, why it needs to be solved, and why the solution(s) is important in the big picture;
- Begins with a clear, analytical thesis statement that summarizes both the problem and the possible solution(s);
- Includes at least three appropriate supporting ideas;
- Uses pertinent evidence to support argument; and
- Employs relevant transition language to effectively lead the reader through the argument.

Zone of Proximal Development

The essay includes only a partial thesis statement and/or some supporting evidence.

Significant Reteaching

The essay includes little or no thesis statement, little or no supporting evidence, and does not lead the reader through the argument.

Concept-Definition Structure of Argument Criteria

Exemplary

The essay includes a concise thesis statement, appropriate and well-chosen supporting evidence, and transparently leads the reader through the argument:

- Concisely explains how the concept-definition essay can help someone better understand the concept and why understanding the concept is important in the big picture, making insightful connections in the process;
- Begins with a concise, analytical thesis statement summarizing the definition of the concept;
- Includes at least three appropriate and exceptional supporting ideas;
- Uses pertinent and well-chosen evidence to support argument; and
- Employs accurate transition language to effortlessly lead the reader through the argument.

Proficient

The essay includes a well-defined thesis statement, appropriate supporting evidence, and effectively leads the reader through the argument:

- Clearly explains how the concept-definition essay can help someone better understand the concept and why understanding the concept is important in the big picture;
- Begins with a clear, analytical thesis statement summarizing the definition of the concept;
- Includes at least three appropriate supporting ideas;
- Uses pertinent evidence to support the argument; and
- Employs relevant transition language to effectively lead the reader through the argument.

Zone of Proximal Development

The essay includes only a partial thesis statement and/or some supporting evidence.

Significant Reteaching

The essay includes no thesis statement, no supporting evidence, and does not lead the reader through the argument.

Goal-Action-Outcome Structure of Argument Criteria

Exemplary

The essay includes a concise thesis statement, appropriate and well-chosen supporting evidence, and transparently leads the reader through the argument:

- Concisely explains how the goal-action-outcome essay can help someone better understand how or why something occurs and why it is important in the big picture, making insightful connections in the process;
- Begins with a concise, analytical thesis statement articulating a clear goal and the reason for the goal;
- Includes at least three appropriate and exceptional supporting ideas;
- Uses pertinent and well-chosen evidence to support argument; and
- Employs accurate transition language to effortlessly lead the reader through the argument.

Proficient

The essay includes a well-defined thesis statement, appropriate supporting evidence, and effectively leads the reader through the argument:

- Clearly explains how the goal/action/outcome essay can help someone better understand how or why something occurs and why doing it is important in the big picture;
- Begins with a clear, analytical thesis statement articulating a specific goal and the reason for the goal;
- Includes at least three appropriate supporting ideas;
- Uses pertinent evidence to support argument; and
- Employs relevant transition language to effectively lead the reader through the argument.

Zone of Proximal Development

The essay includes only a partial thesis statement and/or some supporting evidence.

Significant Reteaching

The essay includes little or no thesis statement, little or no supporting evidence, and does not lead the reader through the argument.

Proposition-Support Structure of Argument Criteria

Exemplary

The essay includes a concise thesis statement, appropriate and well-chosen supporting evidence, and transparently leads the reader through the argument:

- Concisely explains how the proposition-support essay can help someone better understand and agree with the proposition and why agreement is important in the big picture, making insightful connections in the process.
- Begins with a concise, analytical thesis statement expressing a clear point of view or opinion.
- Includes at least three appropriate and exceptional supporting ideas;
- Uses pertinent appropriate and well-chosen evidence used to support argument; and
- Employs accurate transition language to effortlessly lead the reader through the argument.

Proficient

The essay includes a well-defined thesis statement, appropriate supporting evidence, and effectively leads the reader through the argument:

- Clearly explains how the proposition-support essay can help someone better understand and agree with the proposition and why agreement is important in the big picture;
- Begins with a clear, analytical thesis statement expressing a clear point of view or opinion;
- Includes at least three appropriate supporting ideas;
- Uses pertinent evidence to support argument; and
- Employs relevant transition language to effectively lead the reader through the argument.

Zone of Proximal Development

The essay includes only a partial thesis statement and/or some supporting evidence.

Significant Reteaching

The essay includes little or no thesis statement, little or no supporting evidence, and does not lead the reader through the argument.

Notes

WRITING IN ALL SUBJECT AREAS

Because writing is thinking, the organization of an individual's writing reflects both the structure of her thinking and the depth of her understanding. Students should be writing (and thinking!) continually, explaining what they know and how they know it. That is why it is essential for *all* teachers in a particular school (or district) to provide students with at least some analytical writing assignments in their classrooms.

The elements of an analytical essay described in this guide are present in *all* non-fiction text structures. However, they may have different names in different subject areas. This chart identifies what each structural element is called in each of the core subjects:

	Thesis Statement (one sentence)	Evidence/Proof	Conclusion	Most Common Text Structures
Literature & Language Arts	Thesis Statement	❖ Quotations from the text(s) ❖ Examples from within and between the text(s) ❖ Analysis by literary critics	Conclusion	Compare-Contrast Concept-Definition Proposition-Support Cause-Effect
History/ Social Studies	Thesis Statement OR Historical Argument	❖ Historical examples from primary source documents ❖ Interpretations from academic historians (secondary sources) ❖ Examples of previous events or predictions based on prior examples	Conclusion OR Historical Interpretation	Cause-Effect Compare-Contrast Concept-Definition Proposition-Support

	Thesis Statement (one sentence)	Evidence/Proof	Conclusion	Most Common Text Structures
Science	Hypothesis:

What is being proven? | ❖ Experimental results of others

❖ Student's own experimental results | Results/ Analysis Conclusion

Was the hypothesis proven or disproven? How and why? | Goal-Action-Outcome (lab report)

Cause-Effect

Compare-Contrast

Concept-Definition |
| Math | Goal Statement:

What is being solved? | ❖ Calculations

❖ Logical proofs (geometry)

❖ Analysis linked using transitional phrases | Outcome Statement (one sentence)

What is the answer to the problem in context? | Goal-Action-Outcome

Cause-Effect

Compare-Contrast

Concept-Definition |

Each subject area involves different terminology and types of supporting evidence and examples. Writing in math, for example, will *not* be a block of text; it will *not* be narrative writing. Instead math texts will be primarily goal-action-outcome. For the most part, a written explanation in math will be only one or two paragraphs. It will begin with a one-sentence goal statement, followed by supporting evidence in the form of calculations and/or proofs, connected by transitional words, and finally an outcome stated in a complete sentence. Writing in math leads the reader through the problem solving so a peer or teacher can understand and correct the thinking, where necessary.

Not all math problems require written answers. Perhaps the last few questions on a test will be complex, real-world application problems like the one below:

Geometry Assignment (figure not to scale)

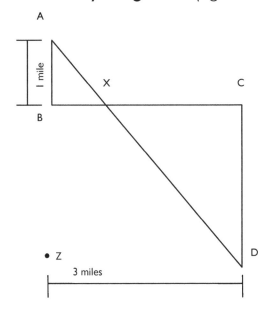

Going from his own house (A) to Raul's house (D), Mark drives due south one mile, due east three miles, and due south again for three miles. What is the distance between the two houses as the crow flies? Explain, in writing and using appropriate math terminology and notation, how to prove that ▲ABX ~ ▲DCX. Use corresponding side lengths of the triangles to calculate BX and use the Pythagorean Theorem to calculate AX and then DX. Then find AD.

Sample Response:

The Pythagorean Theorem and its associated corollaries are critical when finding the distance between two points. In fact, all GPS navigation systems rely on the Pythagorean Theorem to determine location in space. (Lead-in) Although slightly simpler, finding the distance between Raul and Mark's houses uses the Pythagorean Theorem and associated corollaries, in the same way. (Goal Statement) Employing the AA Similarity Postulate to prove that the triangles created on the map are similar allows the use of the Pythagorean Theorem to solve for the exact distance between the two houses. (Statement of Structure)

(Supporting evidence/details)
Proof:

$\triangle ABX$ and $\triangle DCX$ are right triangles; as a result, $\triangle AXB$ and $\triangle CXD$ are vertical angles, therefore similar, according to the AA (angle-angle) Similarity Postulate. Because the sum of all angles in a triangle is always $180°$ and each of these triangles has one right angle and one similar angle, it follows that the third angle in each triangle is also similar. Therefore, $\triangle ABX \sim \triangle DCX$.

In order to find the length of BX, develop a ratio of similar triangles using the measurements that were given in the problem:

$$\frac{1 \text{ mile (AB)}}{BX} = \frac{4 \text{ miles (AZ)}}{3 \text{ miles (CD)}} \rightarrow \quad 1(3) = 4(BX) \quad \rightarrow \quad \frac{3}{4} = BX$$

$$\rightarrow \boxed{BX = \tfrac{3}{4} \text{ miles or .75 miles}}$$

Then, using the Pythagorean Theorem ($a^2+b^2=c^2$), find AX, DX, and AD.

$$(1 \text{ mile})^2 + (\tfrac{3}{4} \text{ miles})^2 = (AX)^2 \rightarrow 1 + 9/16 = (AX)^2 \rightarrow \sqrt{25/16} = \sqrt{(AX)^2}$$

$$\rightarrow \boxed{AX = 5/4 \text{ or } 1.25 \text{ miles}}$$

Continued...

$(3 \text{ miles})^2 + (1.25)^2 = (DX)^2 \rightarrow 9 + 1.56 = (DX)^2 \rightarrow \sqrt{10.56} = \sqrt{(DX)^2}$

$$\rightarrow \boxed{DX = 13/4 \text{ or } 3.25 \text{ miles}}$$

$3^2 + 4^2 = (AD)^2 \qquad \rightarrow \qquad$ this is a 3-4-5 triangle

$$\rightarrow \boxed{AD = 5 \text{ miles}}$$

Therefore, using ratios of similar right triangles and the Pythagorean Theorem, the distance between Raul and Mark's houses as the crow flies is 5 miles. (Outcome Statement)

Writing in Science: The Lab Report

Science lab reports are a specialized goal-action-outcome text structure:

- ❖ **Goal:** To prove or disprove the hypothesis
- ❖ **Action:** The materials and procedures required
- ❖ **Outcome:** The analysis and conclusion

While other text structures can also be used in science, the lab report is the staple of science education. Whenever students do an experiment they should report their results in this format because it remains the same from Kindergarten through graduate school. The only elements of a lab report that change from year to year are the complexity of the experiments and equipment and whether it is original research or the repeat of a famous experiment. The following is a brief description of what must be included in an acceptable lab report:

1 **Identify yourself** and your partner(s)

2 **Title** of the lab/activity. It is **not** a creative title as described in this guide's *Title* section; rather it is purely descriptive:

> The Mean Number of Jumping Jacks Completed by Our Lab Group in One Minute

3 **Purpose**—Why study this problem?
State the objective. What concept or skill is highlighted by this activity? Ask, "Why did we do this? What were we supposed to learn or practice?

4   **Introduction**—What is the problem or issue being addressed?

The introduction to a lab report should identify the problem or issue to be solved or the experiment to be performed and explain its purpose and significance in one or two sentences, providing any necessary background information the reader needs. It ends with an hypothesis; one sentence that specifically states the question the experiment is designed to answer.

Note on Verb Tense:

Introductions often create difficulties for those who struggle with keeping verb tenses straight. These two points should help to navigate the introduction:

❖ The report, the theory, and permanent equipment still exist; therefore, these items are in the present tense: "The purpose of this report **is**...," "Bragg's Law for diffraction **is**...," "The scanning electron microscope **produces** micrographs..."

❖ The experiment has been completed. Use the *past* tense when discussing it. "The objective of the experiment **was**..."

The objective of this experiment was to determine the mean number of jumping jacks completed by our lab group in one minute. (purpose statement)

AND

Our hypothesis is that our group can complete a mean number of 60 jumping jacks in one minute. (hypothesis)

---

5 **Materials**

This section describes how and when students conducted the experiment, including the experimental design (what they did), experimental apparatus (materials), methods of gathering and analyzing data, and types of control. Often these types of information are complied in the form of a table.

Materials:

Stop-watch

Space in which to do jumping jacks

Paper

Pencil

6 **Procedure**—What was done? How was it done?

For the beginner, this is probably the most difficult part of the report. Up to this point in school most student writing has been descriptive. Technical writing, on the other hand, is "cut and dried," conveying a mental picture of what occurred. Write about only what has transpired, so the reader can visualize the set-up. Be sure to include reference to any equipment used (e.g., We used a stop watch to time each person). The instructions must be very specific, though ordinal phrases are not necessary (i.e., first, second, third, etc.), since that information is conveyed by the sentence order in the description. A diagram or picture of the apparatus may be helpful, but it should not replace a good verbal description.

Remember that based on the lab report, members of the audience should be able to repeat the procedure exactly if they are so inclined.

Reminders:

❖ Emotions (This was hard. This was fun.) are not relevant in a lab report.

❖ Fill out lab reports in the past tense because the experiment is finished.

- ❖ Write complete sentences.

- ❖ Use either first person active voice or passive voice to describe the lab procedures.

    First person active voice: I timed each group member.

    Passive voice: Each group member was timed.

7 **Observations & Data (Outcome)**—What were the results?
This section comprises only those aspects of the experiment the student saw, heard, touched, or smelled (*never* taste anything in a science lab). Observations and data are presented without interpretations or conclusions.

Both quantitative (numerical) and qualitative (sensory, *not* emotional) observations are noted. Units are necessary when recording measurements, but a value that cannot be measured directly (such as density) should not be included as data. Quantitative observations are best presented in data tables. Qualitative observations may be organized in table form or paragraph form.

When uncertain whether something should be included ask, "How did I get this piece of information? What instrument did I use to collect this information?" The goal is to present all the data collected in a clear and easily understood format. Well-organized well-written results provide the framework for the discussion section.

Reminders:
- ❖ Record all information in the order the observations were made, writing in complete sentences.

- ❖ Use both words and numbers to define the data, employing proper scientific terminology and units of measure.

- ❖ Tables and graphs supplement the text and present the data in a more understandable form. Raw data is usually supplied in table format, with the highlights summarized in graph form.

❖ The written text of the results section may be as short as one sentence summarizing the salient points and directing the reader to specific tables and figures.

❖ Include results that "went wrong" or were unexpected. This can be useful for someone trying to repeat the experiment.

❖ Sample or detailed calculations for a lab report may be included in either a separate section titled *Calculations* or in an appendix at the end of the report.

8 **Analysis of Data (Discussion)**—What do they mean? How do the results relate to previous work in the field?

This is the section where students show any calculations based on their data. Both the formula and the measurements for each computation must be included, followed by the solution. Once there is a sample calculation, a data table can show other calculated values of the same type. This is also the appropriate place to explain how the measurements relate to each other and discuss anything that happened during the activity that might have affected the data.

Students must explain what they think their collected data mean:

❖ Describe patterns and relationships that emerged;

❖ Discuss what was observed, why it happened (or the most likely reason), and how it relates to the purpose of the experiment;

❖ Compare these results to trends described in the literature and/or by theoretical behavior.

❖ Support interpretations by incorporating course material, the lab manual, and comments from the teacher. For more in-depth discussion, read other resources, like peer-reviewed journal articles. If outside sources are used, reference the information properly.

❖ Write descriptively. Readers might jump to the *Discussion* section first in order to discover what happened, so provide enough information for them to understand what occurred. Remind the reader of the outcome *without* repeating endless details from *Results*.

> **The temperature increased during the second phase because of the drug treatment.** (Discussion Statement)
>
> NOT
>
> **The temperature increased during the second phase.** (repetition of Results Statement)

- ❖ When the *Results* section is well organized, it can be a guide to writing the *Discussion* section. Refer to the same tables and figures to explain the changes/trends/unexpected results.

- ❖ Accept or reject the hypothesis and explain why (it is acceptable to reject an hypothesis that has been proven untrue). If applicable, explain why the results did not turn out as predicted. If something went horribly wrong or was damaged, disturbed, or contaminated; if there were changes to the experimental procedure; or if the equipment was faulty include that information and explain how it may have affected the results.

- ❖ If the lab instructions include questions to be answered in the *Discussion*, integrate the answers into a logical examination, rather than answering them one-by-one. Don't include *only* the answers to the questions—use them as a guideline to supplement discussion, not limit it.

9   Conclusion

This is the section of the lab report where the writer discusses how the purpose of the activity relates to the analysis of the data and how it can be applied to the real world. Conclusions are connections that are not obvious on the surface. In other words, what did the writer learn? Stick to the facts.

This is not the place to comment on whether or not the activity was enjoyable. If the results were not satisfactory, suggest how the activity could be improved to give better data. Were questions raised that cannot be answered? This is the place to mention them. Also, include any recommendations for further research or changes for the next time that might generate more significant or noteworthy results.

10   Tables and Figures (only if required)

Tables and figures are often used in a report to present complicated data. Use the following guidelines to incorporate them effectively.

❖ Tables are referred to as tables. All other items (graphs, photographs, drawings, diagrams, maps, etc.) are referred to as figures.

❖ All tables and figures must be numbered, assigned in the order they are mentioned in the text. However, they are numbered independently of each other (i.e., Table 1 and Table 2, and then Figure 1 and Figure 2).

❖ All tables and figures must include self-explanatory titles so the reader can understand their content without the text:

Table 1. Number of jumping jacks completed by each group member in one minute

❖ Tables are usually labeled at the top and figures at the bottom.

❖ Each table or figure *must* be introduced within the text, summarizing the highlight(s) or significant trends only:

Do not write:
Amy completed 60 jumping jacks in one minute, Joe completed 54 jumping jacks in one minute, Frank completed 57 jumping jacks in one minute, and Jill completed 59 jumping jacks in one minute.

> Simply state:
>
> Members of the group completed different numbers of jumping jacks in one minute (Figure 1).

- ❖ Tables and figures may be placed either at the end of the report, or as soon as possible within the text without causing an interruption (i.e., at the end of a paragraph or section).

- ❖ Avoid referring to "the table below" because often the final placement of the table will be uncertain. Instead, refer to the specific table or figure number; the readers can always find the information.

- ❖ Though tables and figures enhance a report, the reader should be able to understand and follow the results even if they are removed.

Identify yourself: Amy, Joe, Frank, and Jill

Title: The Mean Number of Jumping Jacks Completed by Our Lab
Group in One Minute

Purpose:

The objective of this experiment was to determine the mean number of jumping jacks completed by our lab group in one minute. Our hypothesis is that we will be able to complete a mean number of 60 jumping jacks within that time.

Materials:

- ❖ Stop watch
- ❖ Space in which to do jumping jacks
- ❖ Paper
- ❖ Pencil

Procedure:

1. Clear space to do jumping jacks.
2. Designate one person in the group as the timer.
3. Each person takes a turn being timed doing jumping jacks for one minute.
4. Someone switches places with the timer so that she can be also be timed.
5. Record all the data.
6. Figure out the mean a + b + c + d = x.

   Mean = x ÷ number of students in the group

Observations & Data

Table 1: Number of jumping jacks completed by each student in one minute

Students	Number completed
Amy	60
Joe	54
Frank	57
Jill	59

Each member of the group completed a different number of jumping jacks, but none did fewer than 54 or more than 60 (See Table 1).

Analysis of Data

Each person in the group performed a different number of jumping jacks in one minute. None of us could do more than 60 jumping jacks, so it appears no one can do more than one jumping jack per second. However, the two tallest participants did the most jumping jacks.

60 + 54 + 57 + 59 = 230   230÷4 = 57.5   Mean = 57.5

Conclusion

Our hypothesis was incorrect. The mean number of jumping jacks our group completed in one minute was 57.5, not 60. Even though we are all 12 or 13 years old, we have different physical capabilities. In case the timing was not exact, we should verify our results by repeating the experiment using a different timer. In addition, this lab group could work on its general fitness and try the experiment again to see if that will have an impact on the results.

Tables and Figures

Figure 1. Members of the groups completed different numbers of jumping jacks in one minute.

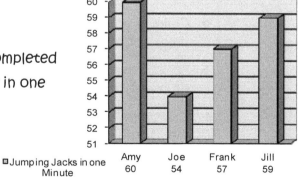

ANALYTICAL WRITING IDEAS FOR NON-CORE SUBJECTS

The core subjects are defined as literature and language arts, history/social studies, science, and mathematics. However, thinking is important across the curriculum. A few formal writing assignments or projects each semester for students in these subjects will further their analytical thinking skills, deepen their content knowledge, and improve their overall achievement. In order to provide a jumpstart, here are some sample topics in other subjects:

SUBJECT	SAMPLE PROMPTS
World Language	❖ Compare and contrast the education systems of the United States and (country). [compare-contrast] ❖ Explain the defining characteristics of the culture of (country). [concept-definition] ❖ Compare and contrast the verb tenses in English and (language). [compare-contrast]
Art	❖ What defines pointillist art? [concept-definition] ❖ What choices did you make when creating your sculpture and why? [concept-definition or proposition-support] ❖ Review the (title) exhibit at the Museum of Modern Art. [proposition-support]
Music	❖ Critique your performance (or the ensemble's performance) of (title). [concept-definition or proposition-support] ❖ Explain the science behind the production of sound in your instrument. [cause-effect] ❖ Compare and contrast how two different instruments playing the same piece of music can convey different moods. [compare-contrast]

SUBJECT	SAMPLE PROMPTS
P.E.	❖ Was the referee/umpire who made the (real-life controversial call) correct or incorrect? Why or why not? [proposition-support] ❖ Define sportsmanship. [concept-definition] ❖ What is the purpose of rules and regulations in sport? [concept-definition or cause-effect]
Health	❖ Describe the path of a cheeseburger as it is digested. Begin in the mouth and end with excretion. Describe where and how each part of the cheeseburger is broken down, identifying all the chemicals and enzymes involved. [goal-action-outcome] ❖ Develop a plan to effectively fight childhood obesity. [problem-solution] ❖ Should the use of alternative medicine be covered by medical insurance? Why or why not? [proposition-support]
Philosophy	❖ Is man the creator and mover of his life, or does he live at the mercy of forces over which he has little control? Does free will exist or is how he conducts his life determined by outside factors? [proposition-support or concept-definition] ❖ What is the ideal relationship between the individual and the state? Should the individual serve the state or should the state serve the individual? [proposition-support] ❖ Who should control educating a nation's children? Parents? Students? The state? [proposition-support]
Science, Technology, Engineering & Mathematics (STEM)	❖ How could the heat exchanger on a heat pump be modified to allow someone to heat his pool while at the same time cooling his home? [goal-action-outcome or cause-effect] ❖ Explain how wind turbines work and how they can be used. [goal-action-outcome] ❖ Compare and contrast the inner workings of a refrigerator and a room air conditioner. [compare-contrast]

GO FORTH AND PROSPER

The test of a successful person is not an ability to eliminate all problems before they arise, but to meet and work out difficulties when they do arise. We must be willing to make an intelligent compromise with perfection lest we wait forever before taking action. It's still good advice to cross bridges as we come to them.

—David Joseph Schwartz

Teaching effective analytical writing and thinking is not as easy as some might like, but it is certainly not as hard as many fear. The pieces have been broken down and explained. Now the effort is up to all of you.

Initially, teachers' instruction and students' products will not be perfect, even with this guide. The only way to become a fluent writer and thinker, and to eventually do much of what is in this guide in one's head, is to practice, practice, practice.

The good news is that if all teachers in a school are working from this guide, the instruction is shared among the staff. It takes more than one educator to provide the amount of information, instruction and practice necessary to significantly improve students' writing and thinking. However, even if you are working alone, this guide is a start. The world is not a perfect place, but we can each do our part in an attempt to make it so.

Please contact Lightbulb Learning Services via www.lightbulblearning.net with any feedback, comments, questions, or concerns. This is an iterative process and I welcome your input as to how to provide students with the skills they will need to succeed.

Even a journey of a thousand miles begins with one step. Let's start!